lonely planet

AMALFI COAST

ROAD TRIPS

Cristian Bonetto,
Brendan Sainsbury

HOW TO USE THIS BOOK

Reviews

In the Destinations section:

All reviews are ordered in our authors' preference, starting with their most preferred option. Additionally:

Sights are arranged in the geographic order that we suggest you visit them and, within this order, by author preference.

Eating and Sleeping reviews are ordered by price range (budget, midrange, top end) and, within these ranges, by author preference.

Map Legend

Routes
▬▬	Trip Route
▬▬	Trip Detour
▬▬	Linked Trip
▬▬	Walk Route
▬▬	Tollway
▬▬	Freeway
	Primary
	Secondary
	Tertiary
	Lane
	Unsealed Road
▨▨	Plaza/Mall
▦▦▦	Steps
)=＝	Tunnel
▭▭▭	Pedestrian Overpass
‐ ‐ ‐	Walk Track/Path

Boundaries
‐ ‐ ‐	International
‐ ‐ ‐	State/Province
▬▬▬	Cliff

Hydrography
	River/Creek
	Intermittent River
	Swamp/Mangrove
	Canal
	Water
	Dry/Salt/ Intermittent Lake
	Glacier

Highway Markers
A6	Autostrada
SS231	State Highway
SR203	Regional Highway
SP3	Provincial Highway
E74	Other Road

Trips
1	Trip Numbers
9	Trip Stop
⬆	Walking tour
↱	Trip Detour

Population
✪	Capital (National)
◉	Capital (State/Province)
●	City/Large Town
●	Town/Village

Areas
	Beach
	Cemetery (Christian)
	Cemetery (Other)
	Park
	Forest
	Reservation
	Urban Area
	Sportsground

Transport
✈	Airport
⊶⊕⊶	Cable Car/ Funicular
Ⓜ	Metro station
Ⓟ	Parking
⊶⊕⊶	Train/Railway
⊶⊕⊶	Tram

Note: Not all symbols displayed above appear on the maps in this book

---

Symbols In This Book

✓	Top Tips	🍷	Food & Drink
§	Link Your Trips	🌳	Outdoors
○	Tips from Locals	📷	Essential Photo
↱	Trip Detour	🏃	Walking Tour
📖	History & Culture	🍴	Eating
👪	Family	🛏	Sleeping

- - - - - - - - - - - - - - - - - -

👁	**Sights**	🛏	**Sleeping**
🏖	**Beaches**	🍴	**Eating**
🏃	**Activities**	🍷	**Drinking**
📖	**Courses**	☆	**Entertainment**
☞	**Tours**	🔒	**Shopping**
🎊	**Festivals & Events**	ℹ	**Information & Transport**

- - - - - - - - - - - - - - - - - -

These symbols and abbreviations give vital information for each listing:

☎	Telephone number	🐾	Pet-friendly
⊘	Opening hours	🚌	Bus
Ⓟ	Parking	⛴	Ferry
⊝	Nonsmoking	🚋	Tram
✳	Air-conditioning	🚆	Train
@	Internet access	apt	apartments
🛜	Wi-fi access	d	double rooms
🏊	Swimming pool	dm	dorm beds
🌱	Vegetarian selection	q	quad rooms
		r	rooms
🍴	English-language menu	s	single rooms
		ste	suites
👪	Family-friendly	tr	triple rooms
		tw	twin rooms

CONTENTS

Amalfi (p92), Amalfi Coast

WELCOME TO
THE AMALFI COAST

Naples, Pompeii and the Amalfi Coast are the Italy of your wildest dreams – a rich, hypnotic mix of vibrant street life, decadent palaces, pastel-hued villages and aria-inspiring vistas.

With a car you'll discover there's more to Italy than Michelangelo masterpieces and Roman ruins, and you'll be able to properly explore Campania's rugged mountains, steaming fumaroles and ethereal coastal grottoes. Welcome to Italy at its most seductive and intense.

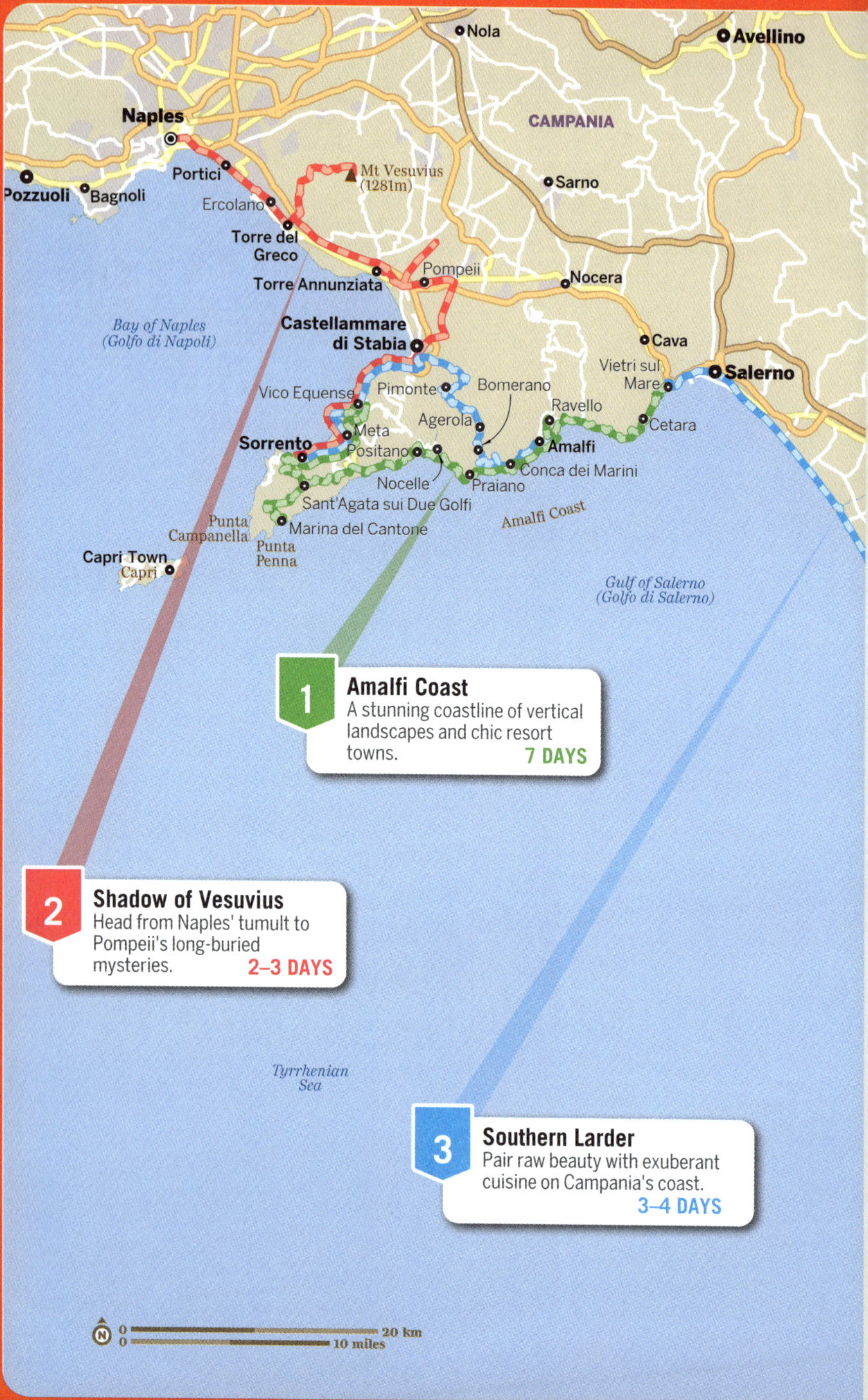

Nola

Avellino

CAMPANIA

Naples

Portici

Pozzuoli Bagnoli

Ercolano

Sarno

Mt Vesuvius
(1281m)

Torre del
Greco

Pompeii

Nocera

Torre Annunziata

Cava

Castellammare
di Stabia

Vietri sul
Mare

Salerno

Bay of Naples
(Golfo di Napoli)

Vico Equense

Pimonte

Bomerano

Ravello

Agerola

Cetara

Meta

Sorrento

Positano

Amalfi

Nocelle

Conca dei Marini

Praiano

Sant'Agata sui Due Golfi

Amalfi Coast

Punta
Campanella

Marina del Cantone

Punta
Penna

Capri Town

Gulf of Salerno
(Golfo di Salerno)

Capri

Amalfi Coast
A stunning coastline of vertical
landscapes and chic resort
towns.   **7 DAYS**

2 **Shadow of Vesuvius**
Head from Naples' tumult to
Pompeii's long-buried
mysteries.   **2–3 DAYS**

Tyrrhenian
Sea

3 **Southern Larder**
Pair raw beauty with exuberant
cuisine on Campania's coast.
             3–4 DAYS

N   0   20 km
    0   10 miles

AMALFI COAST ★

Montecorvino

Monti Picentini

Eboli

Battipaglia

Sele

Altavilla
Silentina

Sicignano
degli Alburni

Grotte
dell'Angelo
Pertosa

BASILICATA

Controne
Grotta di
Castelcivita

Sant'Angelo
a Fasanella

Capaccio
Scalo

Paestum

Castel San
Lorenzo

Bellosguardo

Roscigno
Vecchia

Teggiano

Valle di Diano

**Sala
Consilina**

Padula

Agropoli

Cilento

CAMPANIA

Valle delle
Orchideo

Santa Maria di
Castellabate

Laureana
Cilento

Parco Nazionale
del Cilento e
Vallo di Diano

Castellabate

Punta
Licosa

Vallo della
Lucania

Sanza

Pioppi

Acciaroli

Velia

Ascea

Costiera Cilentana

Pisciotta

Sapri

Golfo di
Policastro

Palinuro

Grotta
Azzurra

Camerota

San Giovanni
a Piro

Marina di
Camerota

4 **Cilento Coastal Trail**
A rugged peninsula where
mountains meet the pristine
sea. **4–5 DAYS**

AMALFI COAST

HIGHLIGHTS

★

WITR/SHUTTERSTOCK ©

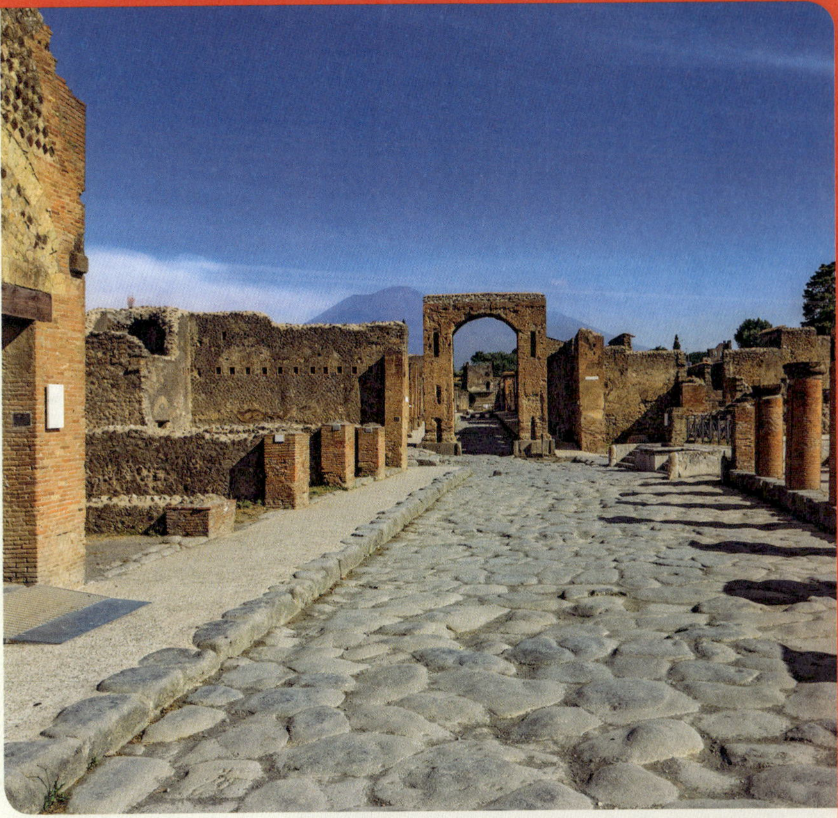

LEOKS/SHUTTERSTOCK ©

Positano (left) Pearl of the Amalfi Coast, Positano is scandalously stunning, a picture-perfect composition of pastel-coloured houses tumbling down towards a deep indigo sea. See it on Trip 1

Pompeii (above) The ruins of Pompeii are a haunting reminder of Mother Nature's merciless force and the fleeting nature of life itself. See it on Trip 2

Amalfi (right) Legendary Amalfi town sparkles the brightest among the glittering string of coastal gems. See it on Trips 1 3

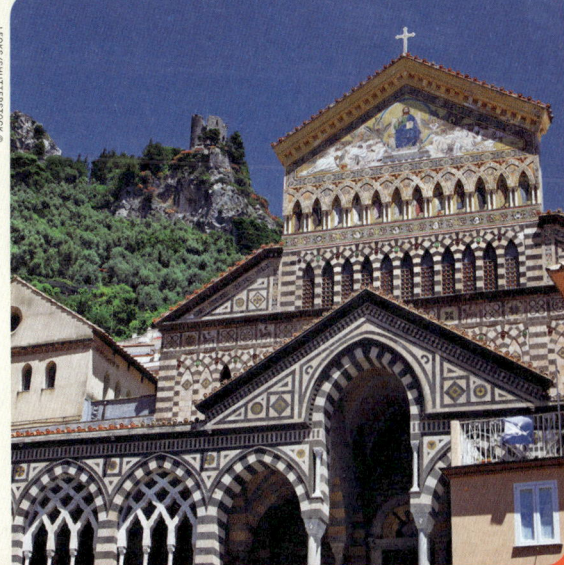

CITY GUIDE

NAPLES

Naples (Napoli) is an exhilarating sprawl of bombastic baroque churches, Dickensian alleyways and electrifying street life. Its in-your-face vitality can be overwhelming, but once you've found your feet you'll discover a city of regal palaces, world-renowned museums, superb pizzerias and sweeping seascapes.

Fruit and vegetables for sale, La Pignasecca

Getting Around

Driving is not the best way of getting around Naples – the roads are anarchic and much of the city centre is off-limits to nonresident traffic. You'll be better off leaving your car as soon as you can and using public transport (bus, metro and funicular); a day pass costs €3.50.

Parking

Street parking is not a good idea – car theft is a problem – and few hotels offer it. There's a 24-hour car park east of the city centre at Via Brin; otherwise ask your hotel for advice.

Where to Eat

To taste authentic Neapolitan pizza, head to the *centro storico* (historic centre) where you'll find a number of hard-core pizzerias serving the genuine article. For a more refined meal, make for seafront Santa Lucia and the cobbled lanes of Chiaia.

Where to Stay

For maximum atmosphere, consider the *centro storico*. Seaside Santa Lucia is home to some of the city's most prestigious hotels, and Chiaia is cool and chic. For lofty views and a chilled-out vibe, hit Vomero.

Useful Websites

I Naples (www.inaples.it) The city's official tourist-board site.

Napoli Unplugged (www.napoliunplugged.com) Up-to-date listings, articles and blog entries.

Road Trip Through Naples: 2

Destination coverage: p54

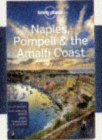

TOP EXPERIENCES

➡ Cappella Sansevero

Marvel at human ingenuity in the Capella Sansevero, a baroque chapel where you'll find Giuseppe Sanmartino's amazing sculpture *Cristo velato* (Veiled Christ).

➡ Museo Archeologico Nazionale

Eye up classical interiors and erotica at the Museo Archeologico Nazionale, which hosts one of the world's finest collections of Graeco-Roman artefacts.

➡ Teatro San Carlo

Demand an encore at Italy's grandest opera house, which regularly stages opera, ballet and concerts.

➡ Museo di Capodimonte

The Museo di Capodimonte might hold one of Italy's less famous collections, but it's also one of its best, showcasing names such as Raphael, Titian, Caravaggio, Masaccio and El Greco.

➡ Certosa e Museo di San Martino

This charterhouse-turned-museum combines cloisters and carriages with romantic views.

➡ Neapolitan Street Life

There's nothing like waking up to the sound of a Neapolitan street market, whether it's rough-and-ready Mercato di Porta Nolana or the city's oldest, La Pignasecca.

MARCOBRIVIO PHOTO/SHUTTERSTOCK ©

NEED TO KNOW

CURRENCY
Euro (€)

LANGUAGE
Italian

VISAS
Generally not required for stays of up to 90 days (or at all by EU nationals). Some nationalities will need a Schengen visa.

FUEL
Filling stations are widespread. Expect to pay around €1.46 per litre of unleaded petrol *(benzina senza piombo)*, €1.29 for diesel *(gasolio)*.

RENTAL CARS
Avis (www.avisautono leggio.it)

Europcar (www.europcar.it)

Hertz (www.hertz.it)

Maggiore (www.maggiore.it)

IMPORTANT NUMBERS
Emergencies (Police 112, 113; Ambulance 115)

Roadside Assistance (803116 from an Italian landline or mobile phone; 800 116800 from a foreign mobile phone)

Climate

Dry climate
Warm to hot summer, mild winter
Warm to hot summer, cold winter
Mild summer, cold winter
Cold climate

Rome
GO Apr–May,
Jul & Nov–Dec

Naples
GO May–Jun
& Sep

When to Go

High Season (Jul–Aug)
» Prices high on the coast; accommodation discounts available in some cities in August.

» Prices also rocket for Christmas, New Year and Easter.

Shoulder (Apr–Jun & Sep–Oct)
» Good deals on accommodation, especially in the south.

» Spring is best for festivals, flowers and local produce.

» Autumn provides warm weather and the grape harvest.

Low Season (Nov–Mar)
» Prices up to 30% lower than in high season.

» Many sights and hotels closed in coastal and mountainous areas.

» A good period for cultural events in large cities.

Your Daily Budget

Budget:
Less than €100
» Dorm bed: €20–35

» Double room in a budget hotel: €60–110

» Pizza or pasta: €6–15

Midrange: €100–250
» Double room in a hotel: €100–200

» Local restaurant dinner: €25–45

» Admission to museum: €4–18

Top End:
More than €250
» Double room in a four- or five-star hotel: €200 plus

» Top restaurant dinner: €45–150

» Opera ticket: €40–210

Eating

Ristorante Formal dining, often with comprehensive wine list and more sophisticated local or national fare.

Trattoria Informal, family-run restaurant cooking up traditional regional dishes.

Vegetarians Most places offer good vegetable starters and side dishes.

Price indicators for a two-course meal with a glass of house wine and *coperto* (cover charge).

€	less than €25
€€	€25–45
€€€	more than €45

Sleeping

Hotels From luxury boutique palaces to modest family-run *pensioni* (small hotels).

B&Bs Rooms in restored farmhouses, city townhouses or seaside bungalows.

Agriturismi Farm stays range from working farms to luxury rural retreats.

Room Tax A nightly occupancy tax is charged on top of room rates.

Price indicators for a double room with private bathroom:

€	less than €110
€€	€110–200
€€€	more than €200

Arriving in Italy

Naples International Airport (Capodichino)
Rental cars Agencies in the Arrivals hall.

Buses Run frequently between 6am and 11.20pm; €5.

Taxis Set fares €18 to €27; 20 to 35 minutes.

Fiumicino (Leonardo da Vinci) Airport (Rome)
Rental cars Agencies are located near the car park.

Trains Run frequently from 6.08am to 11.23pm; €14.

Buses Operate between 6.05am and 12.40am, limited night bus services; €6 to €7.

Taxis Set fare €48; 45 minutes.

Malpensa Airport (Milan)
Rental cars Agencies in the Arrivals halls.

Trains Run half-hourly from 5.37am to 12.20am; €13.

Buses Run every 30 minutes from 3.45am to 12.15am; €10.

Taxis Set fare €95; 50 minutes.

Mobile Phones

Local SIM cards can be used in European, Australian and some unlocked US phones. Other phones must be set to roaming.

Internet Access

Free wi-fi is available in most hotels, hostels, B&Bs and *agriturismi*, and in many bars and cafes.

Money

ATMs are widespread in Italy. Major credit cards are widely accepted, but some smaller shops, trattorias and hotels might not take them.

Tipping

Not obligatory but round up the bill or leave a euro or two in pizzerias and trattorias; 5% to 10% in smart restaurants.

Useful Websites

Lonely Planet (www.lonelyplanet.com/italy) Destination information, hotel bookings and more.

ENIT (www.italia.it) Official Italian-government tourism website.

For more, see Road Trip Essentials (p114).

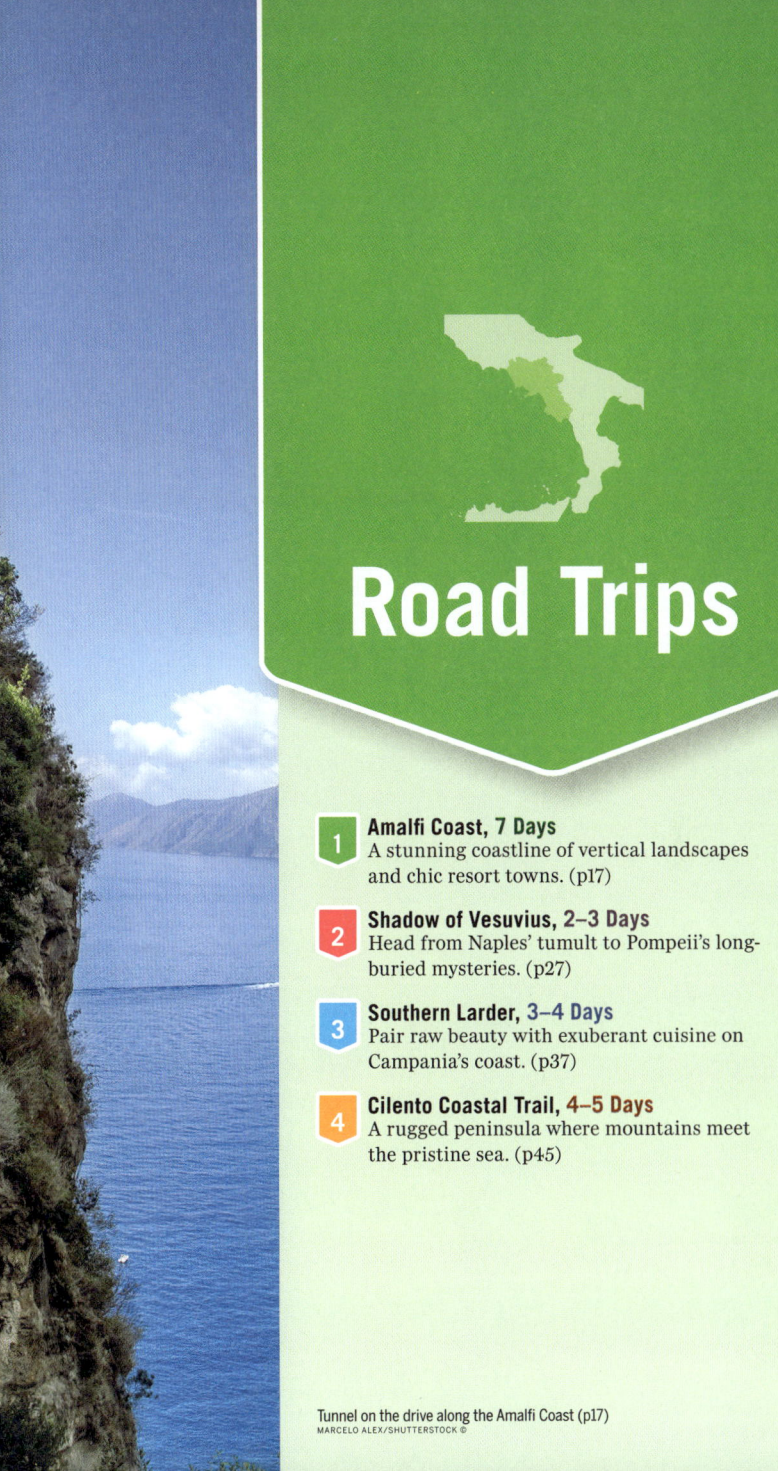

Road Trips

Tunnel on the drive along the Amalfi Coast (p17)
MARCELO ALEX/SHUTTERSTOCK ©

Amalfi Coast

Not for the faint-hearted, this trip along the Amalfi Coast tests your driving skill on a 100km stretch, featuring dizzying hairpin turns and pastel-coloured towns draped over sea-cliff scenery.

TRIP HIGHLIGHTS

25 km

Sant'Agata sui Due Golfi
The region's most panoramic views

83 km

Ravello
Romantic gardens and ethereal coastal views

FINISH
Vietri sul Mare

START
● **Vico Equense**

5

9

8

3

● **Marina del Cantone**

● **Praiano**

76 km

Amalfi
Sun-filled piazzas and a cosmopolitan cathedral

Positano
One of Italy's chicest, most photogenic coastal towns

60 km

7 DAYS
100KM / 62 MILES

GREAT FOR...

BEST TIME TO GO
June or September for beach weather without the peak summer crowds.

 **ESSENTIAL PHOTO**
Positano's vertiginous stack of pastel-coloured houses cascading down to the sea.

☑ **BEST FOR OUTDOORS**
Hiking Ravello and its environs.

1 Amalfi Coast

This trip is all about dramatic landscapes, taking you where mountains plunge seaward in a stunning vertical landscape of precipitous crags, forests and fabled fishing towns. Stops include the celebrated coastal resorts of Positano and Amalfi, as well as serene, mountain-top Ravello, famed for its gardens and views. Cars are useful for inland exploration, as are the walking trails that provide a wonderful escape from the built-up coastal clamour.

❶ Vico Equense (p82)

The Bay of Naples is justifiably famous for its pizza, invented here as a savoury way to highlight two local specialities: mozzarella and sun-kissed tomatoes. Besides its pretty *centro storico* (historic centre), this little clifftop town overlooking the Bay of Naples claims some of the region's top pie, including a by-the-metre version at cult-status **Ristorante & Pizzeria da Gigino** (☎081 879 83 09; www.pizzametro.it; Via Nicotera 15; pizza per metre €28-38; ⏰noon-1.30am; 📶♿).

The Drive » From Vico Equense to Sorrento, your main route will be the SS145 roadway for 12km. Expect to hug the sparkling coastline after Marina di Equa before venturing inland around Meta.

❷ Sorrento (p72)

With its laid-back southern-Italian charm, Sorrento is an appealing holiday town that persistently resists overdevelopment. The *centro storico* is a busy hub for eating, drinking and shopping.

According to Greek legend, it was in Sorrento's waters that the mythical sirens once lived. Sailors of antiquity were powerless to resist the beautiful song of these charming maidens-cum-monsters, who would lure them to their doom.

The Drive » Take the SS145 for 8km to Sant'Agata sui Due Golfi. Sun-dappled village streets give way to forest as you head further inland.

TRIP HIGHLIGHT

❸ Sant'Agata sui Due Golfi (p80)

Perched high in the hills above Sorrento, sleepy Sant'Agata sui Due Golfi commands spectacular views of the Bay of Naples on one side and the Gulf of Salerno on the

LINK YOUR TRIP

2 Shadow of Vesuvius

Follow the curve of the Bay of Naples, from simmering Vesuvius to loud, gregarious Naples.

3 Southern Larder

From Sorrento to Paestum, this trip savours the flavours of Campania's bountiful coast.

other (hence its name, Saint Agatha on the Two Gulfs).

The best viewpoint is the **Convento del Deserto** (Monastero di San Paolo; ☎081 878 01 99; Via Deserto; ☺grounds 8am-7pm, viewpoint 10am-noon & 5-7pm summer, 10am-noon & 3-5pm winter), a Carmelite convent 1.5km uphill from the village centre. It's a knee-wearing hike, but make it to the top and you're rewarded with fabulous 360-degree vistas.

The Drive 》 From Sant'Agata sui Due Golfi to Marina del Cantone it's a 9km drive, the last part involving some serious hairpin turns. Don't let the gorgeous sea views distract you.

❹ Marina del Cantone (p81)

From **Nerano**, where you'll park, a beautiful hiking trail leads down to the stunning Bay of Ieranto and one of the coast's top swimming spots, Marina del Cantone. This unassuming village with its small pebble beach is a lovely, tranquil place to stay as well as a popular diving destination.

The village also has a reputation as a gastronomic hotspot and VIPs regularly catch a boat over from Capri to dine on superlative seafood at **Lo Scoglio** (☎081 808 10 26; www.hotelloscoglio.com; Piazza delle Sirene 15, Marina del Cantone; meals €60; ☺12.30-5pm & 7.30-11pm).

The Drive 》 First, head back up that switchback to Sant'Agata sui Due Golfi. Catch the SS145 and then the SS163 as they weave their way along bluffs and cliff sides to Positano. Most of the 24km offer stunning sea views.

TRIP HIGHLIGHT

❺ Positano (p85)

The pearl in the pack, Positano is the coast's most photogenic and expensive town. Its steeply stacked houses are a medley of peaches, pinks and terracottas, and its near-vertical streets (many of which are, in fact, staircases) are lined with voguish shop displays, elegant hotels and smart restaurants. Look closely, though, and you'll find reassuring signs of everyday reality – crumbling stucco, streaked paintwork and occasionally a faint whiff of problematic drainage.

John Steinbeck visited in 1953 and was so bowled over that he wrote of its dreamlike qualities in an article for *Harper's Bazaar*.

The Drive 》 From Positano to Praiano it's a quick 6km spin on the SS163, passing Il San Pietro di Positano at the halfway point, then heading southeast along the peninsula's edge.

❻ Praiano (p91)

An ancient fishing village, a low-key summer resort and, increasingly, a popular centre for the arts, Praiano is a delight. With no centre as such, its whitewashed houses pepper the verdant ridge of Monte Sant'Angelo as it slopes towards Capo Sottile. Exploring

WALK OF THE GODS

Probably the best-known walk on the Amalfi Coast is the **Sentiero degli Dei**, which follows the high ridge linking Bomerano to Positano. An alternative starting point commences in the heart of **Praiano**, where a thigh-challenging 1000-step start takes you up to the path itself. The route proper is not advised for vertigo sufferers: it's a spectacular, meandering trail along the top of the mountains, with caves and terraces set dramatically in the cliffs and deep valleys framed by the brilliant blue of the sea. You'll eventually emerge at Nocelle, from where a series of steps will take you through the olive groves and deposit you on the road just east of **Positano**. For more information about this walk, see p94.

involves lots of steps and there are several trails that start from town, including the legendary **Sentiero degli Dei**.

For those who'd rather venture below sea level, **La Boa** (📞089 81 30 34; www.laboa.com; Marina di Praia; 1 dive €70) runs dives that explore the area's coral, marine life and grottoes.

The Drive » From Praiano, Marina di Furore is just 3km further on, past beautiful coves that cut into the shoreline.

7 Marina di Furore (p92)

A few kilometres further on, Marina di Furore sits at the bottom of what's known as the fjord of Furore, a giant cleft that cuts through the Lattari mountains. The main village, however, stands 300m above, in the upper Vallone del Furore. A one-horse place that sees few tourists, it breathes a distinctly rural air despite the presence of colourful murals and unlikely modern sculpture.

The Drive » From Marina di Furore to Amalfi, the sparkling Mediterranean Sea will be your escort as you drive eastward along the SS163 coastal road for 6km. Look for Vettica Minore and Conca dei Marini along the way, along with fluffy bunches of fragrant cypress trees.

DETOUR: NOCELLE

Start: 5 **Positano**

A tiny, still relatively isolated mountain village above Positano, Nocelle (450m) commands some of the most memorable views on the entire coast. A world apart from touristy Positano, it's a sleepy, silent place where not much ever happens, nor would its few residents ever want it to. If you want to stay, consider delightful **Villa della Quercia** (📞089 812 34 97; http://villalaquercia.com; Via Nocelle 5; d €75-85; 🕐Apr–mid-Oct; 📶), a former monastery with spectacular vistas. Nocelle lies eight very winding kilometres northeast of Positano.

> ## THE BLUE RIBBON DRIVE
>
> Stretching from Vietri sul Mare to Sant'Agata sui Due Golfi near Sorrento, the SS163 – nicknamed the Nastro Azzurro (Blue Ribbon) – remains one of Italy's most breathtaking roadways. Commissioned by Bourbon king Ferdinand II and completed in 1853, it wends its way along the Amalfi Coast's entire length, snaking round impossibly tight curves, over deep ravines and through tunnels gouged out of sheer rock. It's a magnificent feat of civil engineering – although it can be challenging to drive – and in certain places it's not wide enough for two cars to pass, a fact John Steinbeck alluded to in a 1953 essay.

TRIP HIGHLIGHT

8 Amalfi (p92)

It is hard to grasp that pretty little Amalfi, with its sun-filled piazzas and small beach, was once a maritime superpower with a population of more than 70,000. For one thing, it's not a big place – you can easily walk from one end to the other in about 20 minutes. For another, there are very few historical buildings of note. The explanation is chilling – most of the old city, along with its populace, simply slid into the sea during an earthquake in 1343.

One happy exception is the striking **Cattedrale di Sant'Andrea** (📞089 87 35 58; Piazza del Duomo; 🕐7.30am-8.30pm, closed Nov-Mar), parts of which date from the early 10th century. Between 10am and 5pm entrance to the cathedral is through the

WHY THIS IS A CLASSIC TRIP
CRISTIAN BONETTO, WRITER

From Richard Wagner to Gore Vidal, the Amalfi Coast has bewitched some of the world's most illustrious figures. This is Italy's most arresting coastline, with a natural beauty that borders on the ethereal. While this trip takes in the fabled, sun-drenched towns the Amalfi Coast is famous for, it also sees you hitting the sleepy, hike-friendly hills above, where the views demand a symphony.

Above: Amalfi (p21)
Left: Buffalo mozarella
Right: Ravello

adjacent **Chiostro del Paradiso** (☎089 87 13 24; Piazza del Duomo; adult/reduced €3/1; ☷9am-7.45pm Jul & Aug, reduced hours Sep-early Jan & Mar-Jun, closed early Jan-Feb), a 13th-century Moorish-style cloister.

Be sure to take the short walk around the headland to neighbouring **Atrani**, a picturesque tangle of whitewashed alleys and arches centred on a lively, lived-in piazza and popular beach.

The Drive » Start the 7km trip to Ravello by heading along the coast to Atrani. Here turn inland and follow the SR373 as it climbs the steep hillside in a series of second-gear hairpin turns up to Ravello.

- - - - - - - - - - - - - - - -

TRIP HIGHLIGHT

❾ Ravello (p97)

Sitting high in the hills above Amalfi, polished Ravello is a town almost entirely dedicated to tourism. With impeccable artistic credentials – Richard Wagner, DH Lawrence and Virginia Woolf all lounged here – it's known today for its ravishing gardens and stupendous views, the best in the world according to former resident the late Gore Vidal.

To enjoy these views, head south of Ravello's cathedral to the 14th-century tower that marks the entrance to **Villa Rufolo** (☎089 85 76 21; www.villarufolo.it; Piazza

DETOUR: RAVELLO WALKS

Start: ⑨ **Ravello**

Ravello is the starting point for numerous walks that follow ancient paths through the surrounding Lattari mountains. If you've got the legs for it, you can walk down to **Minori** via an attractive route of steps, hidden alleys and olive groves, passing the picturesque hamlet of **Torello** en route. Alternatively, you can head the other way, to Amalfi, via the ancient village of **Scala**. Once a flourishing religious centre with more than 100 churches and the oldest settlement on the Amalfi Coast, Scala is now a pocket-sized, sleepy place where the wind whistles through empty streets, and locals go patiently about their daily chores.

Duomo; adult/reduced €7/5; ⊙9am-9pm summer, reduced hours winter, tower museum 10am-7pm summer, reduced hours winter). Created by Scotsman Scott Neville Reid in 1853, these gardens combine celestial panoramic views, exotic colours, artistically crumbling towers and luxurious blooms.

Also worth seeking out is the wonderful **Camo** (☎089 85 74 61; www.museo delcorallo.com; Piazza Duomo 9, Ravello; ⊙10am-noon & 3-4pm Mon-Sat). Squeezed between tourist-driven shops, this very special place is, on the face of it, a cameo shop. But don't stop here; ask to see the treasure trove of a museum beyond the showroom.

The Drive » Head back down to the SS163 for a 19km journey that twists and turns challengingly along the coast to Cetara. Pine trees and a variety of flowering shrubs line the way.

⑩ Cetara (p102)

Cetara is a pretty fishing village with a reputation as a gastronomic delight. Since medieval times it has been an important fishing centre, and today its deep-sea tuna fleet is considered one of the Mediterranean's most important. At night, fishermen set out in small boats armed with powerful lamps to fish for anchovies. No surprise then that tuna and anchovies dominate local menus, including

at **Cetara Punto e Pasta** (☎089 26 11 09; Corso Garibaldi 14; meals €25; ⊙noon-4pm & 7-11.30pm Mon, Wed, Thu & Sun, 11.30am-midnight Fri & Sat), a sterling seafood restaurant near the small harbour.

The Drive » From Cetara to Vietri sul Mare, head northeast for 6km on the SS163 for more twisting, turning and stupendous views across the Gulf of Salerno.

⑪ Vietri sul Mare (p103)

The town of Vietri sul Mare lies at the eastern end of Amalfi's coastal road. Ceramics is the main focus here, with production dating back to Roman times. Today, ceramics shopaholics can get their fix at the **Ceramica Artistica Solimene** (☎089 21 02 43; www.ceramicasolimene. it; Via Madonna degli Angeli 7; ⊙9am-8pm Mon-Fri, 9am-1.30pm & 4-8pm Sat, 9am-1.30pm & 4-7pm Sun), a vast factory outlet with an extraordinary glass and ceramic facade.

For a primer on the history of the area's ceramics, seek out the **Museo della Ceramica** (☎089 21 18 35; Villa Guariglia, Via Nuova Raito; ⊙9am-3pm Tue-Sat, 9.30am-1pm Sun) in the nearby village of Raito.

Right An artisan working clay, Vietri sul Mare

Shadow of Vesuvius

Beginning in the tumult that is Naples, this trip winds around the Bay of Naples to magnificent Roman ruins and on to Sorrento – even daring the slopes of Vesuvius itself.

TRIP HIGHLIGHTS

0 km

Naples
Incomparable city of magnificent art, architecture and street life

20 km

Mt Vesuvius
A silent time bomb with summit views worthy of fire god Vulcan

1 START

5

10 km

3

Herculaneum
Superbly preserved ruins, from ancient advertisements to terror-struck skeletons

Oplontis

8

55 km

Pompeii
An extraordinary, haunting portal to the 1st century AD

Castellammare di Stabia

Sorrento
FINISH

2–3 DAYS
90KM / 56 MILES

GREAT FOR...

BEST TIME TO GO
Spring and autumn for best weather; December for stunning Christmas displays.

 ESSENTIAL PHOTO
Capture Vesuvius' brooding majesty from Naples' waterfront.

 BEST FOR HISTORY
Relive history amid Herculaneum's ruins.

2 Shadow of Vesuvius

This trip begins in Naples (Napoli), a city that rumbles with contradictions — grimy streets hit palm-fringed boulevards, crumbling facades mask golden baroque ballrooms. Rounding the Bay of Naples and the dense urban sprawl, you quickly reach some of the world's most spectacular Roman ruins including Pompeii and Herculaneum, as well as lesser known jewels, from Portici's royal getaway to sprawling ancient villas. Above it all looms Vesuvius' dark beauty.

TRIP HIGHLIGHT

❶ Naples (p54)

Italy's most misunderstood city is also one of its finest – an exhilarating mess of frescoed cupolas, mysterious shrines and catacombs, and boisterous, hyperactive street markets. Contradiction is the catchphrase here. It's a place where anarchy, pollution and poverty share the stage with lavish theatres, glorious museums and cafe-lounging artists and intellectuals.

The Unesco-listed *centro storico* (historic centre) is an intoxicating warren of streets packed with ancient churches, citrus-filled cloisters and first-rate pizzerias. It's here, under the washing lines, that you'll find classic Neapolitan street life – overloaded Vespas hurtling through cobbled alleyways and clued-up *casalinghe* (housewives) bullying market vendors. Move towards the sea and the cityscape opens up. Imperious palaces flank show-off squares and seafront panoramas take in fabled Capri and mighty Vesuvius. This is Royal Naples, the Naples of the Bourbons that so impressed the 18th-century grand tourists.

LINK YOUR TRIP

3 **Southern Larder**
From Sorrento, you can embark on this culinary adventure along the Amalfi Coast and the Gulf of Salerno, where mozzarella rules the roost.

1 **Amalfi Coast**
Vico Equense kicks off this week-long adventure of hairpin turns and vertical landscapes amid the world's most glamorous stretch of coastline.

VESUVIAN WINES

Vesuvian wine has been relished since ancient times. The rare combination of rich volcanic soil and a favourable microclimate created by its slopes makes the territory one of Italy's most interesting viticultural areas. Lacryma Christi (literally 'tears of Christ') is the name of perhaps the most celebrated wine produced on the slopes of Mt Vesuvius.

Further afield, other top regional wines include Taurasi, Fiano di Avellino, Aglianico del Taburno and Greco di Tufo.

To prepare for Pompeii and Herculaneum, head to the **Museo Archeologico Nazionale** (☎848 800288; www.museoarcheologiconapoli.it; Piazza Museo Nazionale 19; adult/reduced €15/2; ⊙9am-7.30pm Wed-Mon; Ⓜ Museo, Piazza Cavour). With one of the world's finest collections of Graeco-Roman artefacts, it stars a series of stunning sculptures, mosaics from Pompeii, and a room full of ancient erotica.

The Drive » A straight 8km drive along the SS18 provides a relatively easy journey from central Naples straight to the Palazzo Reale di Portici – if the other drivers behave, of course.

- - - - - - - - - - - - - - - - - -

② **Portici**

The town of Portici lies at the foot of Mt Vesuvius and had to be rebuilt in the wake of its ruin by the 1631 eruption. Charles III of Spain, king of Naples and Sicily, erected a stately royal palace here between 1738 and 1748. Known as the **Reggia di Portici** (☎081 253 20 16; www.centromusa.it; Via Università 100, Portici; adult/reduced €5/3; ⊙3-6.30pm Thu, 9.30am-6.30pm Fri-Sun; Botanic Garden closes 1hr before sunset in winter), the palace today houses a couple of worthwhile museums, most notably the **Herculanense Museum** with artefacts from Pompeii and Herculaneum. Even if the museum is closed, the palace is worth a stop for its string of colourfully frescoed rooms. Outside, the exquisite **botanic gardens** are operated by the University of Naples Federico II.

The Drive » The entrance to the ruins of Herculaneum lie just down the street, a couple of kilometres down the SS18.

- - - - - - - - - - - - - - - - - -

TRIP HIGHLIGHT

③ **Herculaneum (p64)**

The ruins of ancient **Herculaneum** (☎081 777 70 08; http://ercolano.beniculturali.it; Corso Resina 187, Ercolano;

adult/reduced €13/2; ⊗8.30am-7.30pm, last entry 6pm Apr-Oct, 8.30am-5pm, last entry 3.30pm Nov-Mar; P) are smaller, less daunting and easier to navigate than Pompeii. They also include some of the area's richest archaeological finds, offering a rare, intimate glimpse of daily life as it was when the Romans ruled the region.

Heavily damaged by an earthquake in AD 63, Herculaneum was completely submerged by the AD 79 eruption of Mt Vesuvius. However, because it was much closer to the volcano than Pompeii, it drowned in a sea of mud, fossilising the town and ensuring that even delicate items were discovered remarkably well preserved.

Seek out the **Casa d'Argo** (Argus House) a well-preserved example of a Roman noble family's house, complete with porticoed garden and *triclinium* (dining area). **Casa dei Cervi** (House of the Stags) is an imposing example of a Roman noble's villa, with two storeys ranged around a central courtyard and animated with murals and still-life paintings. And don't miss the **Terme del Foro** (Forum Baths), with deep pools, stucco friezes and, in the female *apodyterium* (changing room), a striking mosaic of a naked Triton.

The Drive » The museum is only 10km from Herculaneum. Keep heading down the SS18 until you reach the centre of Torre del Greco, where you will turn left on Via Vittorio Veneto, which will quickly turn into Via Guglielmo Marconi. Follow the signs as you wind your way up the lower elevations of Mt Vesuvius, and the Bay of Naples comes into view.

----

4 Museo dell'Osservatorio Vesuviano

Halfway up Mt Vesuvius, this **museum** (Museum of the Vesuvian Observatory; ☏081 610 85 60; www.ov.ingv. it; Via dell'Osservatorio; ⊗by reservation 9.30am-4pm Mon-Sat, from 10am Sun) contains an interesting array of artefacts telling the history of 2000 years of Vesuvius-watching. Founded in 1841 to monitor Vesuvius' moods, it is the oldest volcanic observatory in the world.

DETOUR: CAMPI FLEGREI

Start: ❶ **Naples**

Stretching west of Posillipo Hill to the Tyrrhenian Sea, the oft-overlooked Campi Flegrei (Phlegrean Fields) counterbalances its ugly urban sprawl with lush volcanic hillsides and priceless ancient ruins without the crowds. While its Greek settlements are Italy's oldest, its Monte Nuovo is Europe's youngest mountain. It's not every week that a mountain just appears on the scene. At 8pm on 29 September 1538, a crack appeared in the earth near the ancient Roman settlement of Tripergole, spewing out a violent concoction of pumice, fire and smoke over six days. By the end of the week, Pozzuoli had a new 134m-tall neighbour.

Today, Europe's newest mountain is a lush and peaceful nature reserve. Before exploring the Campi Flegrei, stop at the **tourist office** (☏081 526 14 81; www. infocampiflegrei.it; Largo Matteotti 1a; ⊗9am-8pm Mon-Fri, 9am-6pm Sat & Sun; Ⓜ Pozzuoli, Ⓡ Cumana to Pozzuoli) in Pozzuoli to get local information and purchase a €4 cumulative ticket (valid for two days) to four of the area's key sites: the **Anfiteatro Flavio**, the **Parco Archeologico di Baia**, the **Museo Archeologico dei Campi Flegrei** and the **Parco Archeologico di Cuma**.

Villa dei Misteri (p34), Pompeii

To this day, scientists are still constantly monitoring the active volcanoes at Vesuvius, Campi Flegrei and Ischia.

The Drive » It's many more hairpin turns as you make your way along the same road almost to Vesuvius' crater, about 7km away. Views across the Bay of Naples and Campania are magnificent.

TRIP HIGHLIGHT

⑤ Mt Vesuvius (p66)

Since exploding into history in AD 79, **Mt Vesuvius** (☏081 239 56 53; www.parconazionaledelvesuvio. it; crater adult/reduced €10/8;

⊘ crater 9am-6pm Jul & Aug, to 5pm Apr-Jun & Sep, to 4pm Mar & Oct, to 3pm Nov-Feb, ticket office closes 1hr before crater) has blown its top more than 30 times. The most devastating of these was in 1631, and the most recent was in 1944. It is the only volcano on the European mainland to have erupted within the last 100 years. What redeems this lofty menace is the spectacular view from its **crater** – a breathtaking panorama that takes in Naples, its world-famous bay, and part of the Apennine mountains.

The end of the road is the summit car park, from where a shuttle bus reaches the ticket office and entry point further up the volcano. From here, a relatively easy 860m path leads up to the actual summit (allow 25 minutes), best tackled in comfy sneakers and with a jacket in tow (it can be chilly up top, even in summer). When the weather is bad the summit path is shut.

The Drive » The first part of this 21km stretch heads back down Vesuvius the same way you came up. Head all the way down to the A3 motorway, turn left onto it and head southeast.

The villas of Oplontis are just off the Torre Annunziata exit.

6 Oplontis (p66)

Buried beneath the unappealing streets of modern-day Torre Annunziata, **Oplontis** (☎081 857 53 47; www. pompeiisites.org; Via dei Sepolcri, Torre Annunziata; adult/reduced incl Boscoreale €7/2; ◷8.30am-7.30pm, last entry 6pm Apr-Oct, 8.30am-5pm, last entry 3.30pm Nov-Mar; ☒Circumvesuviana to Torre Annunziata) was once a seafront suburb under the administrative control of Pompeii. First discovered in the 18th century, only two of its houses have been unearthed, and only one, **Villa Poppaea**, is open to the public. This villa is a magnificent example of an *otium villa* (a residential building used for rest and recreation), and may once have belonged to Emperor Nero's second wife.

The Drive » This brief 5km jaunt has you once again heading south on the SS18 to SS268 (Via Settetermini), which leads through scruffy Neapolitan suburbs to Boscoreale.

Herculaneum (p29)

7 Boscoreale (p66)

Some 3km north of Pompeii, the archaeological site of **Boscoreale** (☎081 857 53 47; www.pompeiisites. org; Via Settetermini; adult/reduced incl Oplontis €7/2; ◷8.30am-7.30pm, last entry 6pm Apr-Oct, 8.30am-6.30pm, last entry 5pm Nov-Mar; ▣Circumvesuviana to Villa Regina–Antiquarium) displays a 1st-century-BC country villa and an antiquarium that showcases artefacts from Pompeii, Herculaneum and the surrounding region. Note that the villa was closed at the time of writing but the antiquarium was open to visitors.

The Drive » Head straight back down the SS268 for 1.4km back to the SS18, which will take you right up next to the ruins of Pompeii.

TRIP HIGHLIGHT

8 Pompeii (p67)

Nothing piques human curiosity like a mass catastrophe, and few beat the ruins of **Pompeii** (☎081 857 53 47; www. pompeiisites.org; entrances at Porta Marina & Piazza Anfiteatro; adult/reduced €15/2; ◷9am-7.30pm Mon-Fri, from 8.30am Sat & Sun, last entry

PASS TO THE PAST

If you plan on blitzing the archaeological sites around Pompeii, consider purchasing a multi-attraction ticket (adult/reduced €18/2). Valid for three days, the pass includes entry to Pompeii, Boscoreale and Oplontis. The ticket is available at the ticket offices of all three sites.

6pm Apr-Oct, 9am-5.30pm Mon-Fri, from 8.30am Sat & Sun, last entry 3.30pm Nov-Mar; 🚈 Circumvesuviana to Pompei Scavi–Villa dei Misteri), a stark reminder of Vesuvius' malign forces.

Audio guides (€8) are a sensible investment, and a good guidebook will help – try *Pompeii* published by Electa Napoli. To do justice to the site, allow at least three hours.

Highlights include the 1st-century BC **Terme Suburbane**, famous for its risqué frescoes, and the **foro**, ancient Pompeii's main piazza. To the northeast of the *foro*, the **Lupanare** (brothel) harbours a series of erotic frescoes that originally served as a menu for clients. At the far east of the site, the **Anfiteatro** is the oldest known Roman amphitheatre in existence. Over on the opposite side of town, the **Villa dei Misteri**, one of the site's most complete structures, contains the remarkable

fresco *Dionysiac Frieze*. One of the world's largest ancient paintings, it depicts the initiation of a bride-to-be into the cult of Dionysus, the Greek god of wine.

The Drive » The 9km trip from Pompeii begins heading south along the SS145 (Corso Italia). It will take you through a mixture of suburbs and small farms. Ahead, you will see the mountains of the Amalfi Coast rear up. The ancient villas of Stabiae are just east of Corso Italia, off Via Giuseppe Cosenza.

- - - - - - - - - - - - - - - - - - -

9 Castellammare di Stabia (p66)

In modern-day Castellammare di Stabia, **Stabiae** (☎ 081 857 53 47; www.pompeiisites.org; Via Passeggiata Archeologica, Castellammare di Stabia; ⏱ 8.30am-7.30pm, last entry 6pm Apr-Oct, 8.30am-5pm, last entry 3.30pm Nov-Mar; 🚈 Circumvesuviana to Via Nocera) was once a popular resort for wealthy Romans. It stood on the slopes of the Varano hill

overlooking the entire Bay of Naples, and according to ancient historian Pliny it was lined for miles with extravagant villas. You can visit two of these frescoed villas: the 1st-century-BC Villa Arianna and the larger Villa San Marco, said to measure more than 11,000 sq metres.

The Drive » This trip is a bit longer, at 21km, than the last few. Head back to the SS145, which will soon head over to the coast. Enjoy beautiful views over the Bay of Naples as you wind your way past Vico Equense, Meta and Piano di Sorrento to Sorrento.

- - - - - - - - - - - - - - - - - - -

10 Sorrento (p72)

For an unabashed tourist town, Sorrento still manages to preserve the feeling of a civilised coastal retreat. Even the souvenirs are a cut above the norm, with plenty of fine old shops selling ceramics, lacework and marquetry items. It is also the spiritual home of *limoncello,* a delicious lemon liqueur traditionally made from the zest of Femminello St Teresa lemons, also known as Sorrento lemons. Its tart sweetness makes the perfect nightcap, as well as a brilliant flavouring for both sweet and savoury dishes.

Right Anfiteatro, Pompeii

Southern Larder

From the Amalfi Coast to Paestum, this trip packs in both jaw-dropping natural beauty and mouthwatering cuisine built on fresh fish, sun-kissed vegetables and the world's finest mozzarella.

3

TRIP HIGHLIGHTS

0 km

Sorrento
Civilised coastal resort and spiritual home of *limoncello*

119 km

Paestum
Glorious Greek ruins and the world's finest mozzarella

Pimonte

Cetara

START 1

7

6

35 km

Conca dei Marini
Seaside birthplace of the scrumptious *sfogliatella*

10

FINISH

39 km

Amalfi
A medieval naval power famous for its pasta

3–4 DAYS
119KM / 73 MILES

GREAT FOR...

BEST TIME TO GO
Spring for sunny, clear weather; early autumn for abundant produce.

ESSENTIAL PHOTO
Capture the hypnotically terraced cliffs of Agerola at sunset.

BEST FOR FOODIES
Going to mozzarella's source in Paestum.

3
Southern Larder

Breathtaking natural beauty aside, this trip is a gourmand's Elysium. Food lovers flock to the Amalfi and Cilento coasts from across the globe for local specialities such as *limoncello* (lemon liqueur), ricotta-stuffed *sfogliatella* pastries, and wildly creamy mozzarella made from water-buffalo milk. Burn off the extra calories hiking the Amalfi's jaw-dropping coastal trails or clambering over Paestum's robust Greek ruins.

TRIP HIGHLIGHT

❶ Sorrento (p72)

Most people come to seaside Sorrento as a pleasant stopover between Capri, Naples and the Amalfi Coast. And while it does offer dramatic views of the Bay of Naples and an upbeat holiday vibe, visitors converge here for a very specific treat: *limoncello*, a simple lemon liqueur made from the zest of lemons (preferably the local Femminello St Teresa lemons), plus sugar

and grain alcohol. It's traditionally served after dinner in chilled ceramic cups, and its combination of sweetness and biting tartness makes for a satisfying culinary epilogue.

The Drive » Head north on the SS145, including a beautiful stretch along the Bay of Naples, for 12km to Vico Equense.

② Vico Equense (p82)

Known to the Romans as Aequa, Vico Equense is a small clifftop town.

Largely bypassed by international tourists, it's a laid-back, authentic place worth a quick stopover, if only to experience some of the famous pizza served by the metre at the justly celebrated **Ristorante & Pizzeria da Gigino** (☏081 879 83 09; www.pizzametro.it; Via Nicotera 15; pizza per metre €28-38; ◎noon-1.30am; 🛜💧). Save room for some superb, made-from-scratch gelato at **Gabriele** (☏081 879 87 44; www.gabrieleitalia.com; Corso Umberto I 8; gelato from €2; ◎9am-2pm & 4pm-midnight Wed-Mon, daily Jul & Aug), another local institution.

The Drive » From Vico Equense to Pimonte is 18km. You'll again hug the beautiful Bay of Naples for a while, reaching the turnoff for the SR ex SS366 in Castellammare di Stabia. From here, head inland and uphill as you wind your way to Pimonte.

③ Pimonte

Tucked into the mountains in the easternmost end of the Amalfi peninsula, this small rural town is a far cry from the high-rolling coast, with tractors trundling through the narrow streets. Make a point of stopping at **Bar Pasticceria Palummo** (☏081 879 28 63; www.facebook.com/barpasticceriapalummo; Piazza Roma 27, Pimonte; pastries & cakes from €1.20; ◎6.30am-late, closed Tue winter; 💧) for its cult-status *torta palummo*, a delicious concoction of *pan di spagna* (sponge cake) and almond cream. For a satisfying savoury snack, seek out the *taralli noci e provolone del monaco*, crunchy, savoury biscuits made with walnuts and a semi-hard local cheese.

The Drive » The 8km drive from Pimonte to Agerola takes you along a winding road through forested countryside along the SR ex SS366.

LINK YOUR TRIP

2 **Shadow of Vesuvius**

From Sorrento, follow this itinerary in reverse, heading around the Bay of Naples to wander the ruins of Pompeii and Herculaneum, brave the slopes of Vesuvius, and conquer high-energy Naples.

1 **Amalfi Coast**

Vico Equense kicks off this week-long adventure of hairpin turns and vertical landscapes amid one of the world's most glamorous stretches of coastline.

4 Agerola

Agerola is located amid a wide green valley approximately 600m above sea level. It is surrounded by natural forests and offers amazing views of the nearby mountains and Mediterranean Sea. Be sure to make a stop here for the legendary *fior di latte* (cow's-milk mozzarella) and *caciocavallo* (gourd-shaped traditional curd cheese) produced on the fertile slopes around town.

The Drive » From Agerola, hop back on the SR ex SS366 for a quick 2km jaunt to Bomerano, enjoying a forest of beech trees and a backdrop of mountains thickly quilted with pines. You are now in the depths of the verdant Parco Regionale dei Monti Lattari.

5 Bomerano

Just a stone's throw from Agerola, you can easily follow your nose to tiny Bomerano for delicious buffalo-milk yoghurt, an ultra-rich, mildly tangy and creamy treat. While in town, you can also feast your eyes on the ornate ceiling frieze in the 16th-century **Chiesa San Matteo Apostolo** (Piazza Paolo Capasso 56, Bomerano; ☺7.30am-5pm summer, 7.30am-noon & 3-5pm winter).

The Drive » From Bomerano to Conca dei Marini, continue on the same road, SS366, for 9km as it winds dramatically down to the sea, with strategically placed lookouts along the way. You will do more switchbacking down to the town of Conca dei Marini itself.

DETOUR: CAPRI

Start: 1 Sorrento

A mass of limestone rock that rises sheer through impossibly blue water, Capri (*ca*-pri) is the perfect microcosm of Mediterranean appeal – a smooth cocktail of chi-chi piazzas and cool cafes, Roman ruins and rugged seascapes. Need any more reason to go?

OK, here's one more: the *torta caprese*. Back in the 1920s, when an absent-minded baker forgot to add flour to the mix of a cake order, a great dessert was born. Now an Italian chocolate-and-almond (or chocolate-and-walnut) cake that is traditionally gluten-free, it is named for the island of Capri from which it originated. The cake has a thin hard shell covering a moist interior. It is usually covered with a light dusting of fine powdered sugar, and sometimes made with a small amount of Strega or other liqueur. **Alilauro** (☎081 807 18 12; www.alilauro.it) runs up to 12 daily hydrofoils from Sorrento to Capri (€20.70, 20 minutes).

TRIP HIGHLIGHT

6 Conca dei Marini

This charmingly picturesque fishing village has been beloved by everyone from Princess Margaret to Gianni Agnelli, Jacqueline Onassis and Carlo Ponti. Work up an appetite with an excursion to the **Grotta dello Smeraldo** (admission €5; ☺9am-4pm), a seaside cavern where the waters glow an eerie emerald green. Then head back to the town for a *sfogliatella,* a scrumptious shell-shaped, ricotta-stuffed pastry that was probably invented here in the 18th century in the monastery of Santa Rosa. The local pastry is even honoured with its own holiday: the first Sunday in August.

The Drive » Head northeast on the SS163 to the town of Amalfi.

TRIP HIGHLIGHT

7 Amalfi (p92)

A picturesque ensemble of whitewashed buildings and narrow alleyways set around a sun-kissed central piazza, Amalfi is the main centre on the Amalfi Coast. To glean a sense of its medieval history, explore the hidden

ANTON_IVANOV/SHUTTERSTOCK ©

Piazza Sant'Antonino, Sorrento (p38)

lanes that run parallel to the main street, with their steep stairways, covered porticos and historic shrine niches. And of course, gourmets shouldn't miss *scialatielli*. A fresh pasta resembling short, slightly widened strips of *tagliatelle* (ribbon pasta), it is a local speciality, most commonly accompanied by zucchini and mussels or clams, or a simple sauce of fresh cherry tomatoes and garlic.

The Drive » It's about 15km on the SS163 from Amalfi to Cetara. Silver birches and buildings draped in bougainvillea add to the beauty of the drive.

8 Cetara (p102)

A picturesque tumble-down fishing village, Cetara is also a gastronomic highlight. Tuna and anchovies are the local specialities, especially the sauce from the latter. Known as *colatura di alici*, it flavours homemade pasta dishes like *scialatielli* with local yellow tomatoes and ravioli stuffed with buffalo mozzarella at **Cetara Punto e Pasta** (☎089 26 11 09; Corso Garibaldi 14; meals €25; ◷ noon-4pm & 7-11.30pm Mon, Wed, Thu & Sun, 11.30am-midnight Fri & Sat), a humble, affordable

eatery a short walk up from the beach.

The Drive » Head northeast on SS163 for Salerno. En route, colourful wildflowers spill over white stone walls as you travel the sometimes hair-raising 11km along the coast.

9 Salerno (p104)

Salerno may seem like a bland big city after the Amalfi Coast's glut of pretty towns, but the place has a charming, if gritty, individuality, especially around its vibrant *centro storico* (historic centre). Don't miss the **Duomo** (☎089 23 13 87; www.cattedraledisalerno.it;

41

SERGIO MICHELINI/SHUTTERSTOCK ©

Cetara (p41)

Piazza Alfano; 🕙8.30am-8pm Mon-Sat, 8.30am-1pm & 4-8pm Sun), built in the 11th century and graced by a magnificent main entrance, the 12th-century **Porta dei Leoni**.

Salerno is also an excellent place to try *torta di ricotta e pera* (ricotta-and-pear tart). This dessert is an Amalfi Coast speciality, deriving its unique tang from the local sheep's-milk ricotta.

The Drive » Head south on the SP175 and hug the coast all the way. Lush palm and lemon trees and the sparkling sea are your escorts for this 38km drive to Paestum.

- - - - - - - - - - - - - - - -

TRIP HIGHLIGHT

🔟 Paestum (p107)

Work up an appetite amid Paestum's Unesco-listed Greek **temples** (Area Archeologica di Paestum; 📞0828 81 10 23; www. museopaestum.beniculturali. it; adult/reduced incl museum €12/2, ruins only €8/2; 🕙8.30am-7.30pm daily, last entry 6.50pm, museum closed Mon), some of the best-preserved in the world.

Then head to **Tenuta Vannulo** (📞0828 72 78 94; www.vannulo.it; Via G Galilei 101, Capaccio Scalo; 1hr group tour €5; 🕙9.30am-5pm daily, tours 9am-noon Mon-Sat), a 10-minute drive from Paestum, for a superbly soft and creamy mozzarella made from the organic milk of water buffalo. Group tours are available (reservations are essential) but you can also stop just to buy the cheese. Be warned, though, it usually sells out by early afternoon.

Right *Sfogliatella* (p40)

KOUFAX73/GETTY IMAGES ©

3 1214 00936 8382

Cilento Coastal Trail

Following the wild and rugged coastline of the Cilento peninsula, this trip takes in atmospheric fishing villages, fascinating hilltop towns and glorious ruins hailing from the region's ancient Greek past.

4

TRIP HIGHLIGHTS

0 km

Paestum
Three of the world's best preserved Greek temples

67 km

Velia
A sprawl of Greek, Roman and medieval ruins

START

1

Acciaroli

7

8

San Giovanni a Piro

9

Sapri
FINISH

84 km

Pisciotta
Labyrinthine village streets and dizzying views

95 km

Palinuro
A laid-back resort with a long, inviting beach

4–5 DAYS
143KM / 89 MILES

GREAT FOR...

BEST TIME TO GO

Spring and autumn for hikers; high summer for beach types.

ESSENTIAL PHOTO

Capture rugged coast and royal-blue sea from hilltop Pisciotta.

BEST FOR HISTORY

Paestum's magnificent ancient Greek temples.

4 Cilento Coastal Trail

Barely accessible by road until the 20th century, the jagged cliff-bound Cilento peninsula is one of Italy's least-explored stretches of coastline. After flourishing under the Greeks and Romans, the Cilento was abandoned for centuries to the vagaries of Mediterranean pirates. Today, its fishing villages and pretty hill towns remain largely free of mass development, despite long, sandy beaches, pristine blue waters, and superb local seafood.

TRIP HIGHLIGHT

❶ Paestum (p107)

The three stately, honey-coloured temples at Paestum are among the best preserved in Magna Graecia – the Greek colonies that once held sway over much of southern Italy. The Greeks capitulated to the Romans in 273 BC, and Poseidonia, as it was known, remained a thriving trading port until the fall of the Roman Empire.

Buy tickets to the temples at the **museum**, itself a fascinating repository of frescoes, statues and archaeological artefacts, before entering the site's main entrance.

The first structure you encounter is the 6th-century-BC **Tempio di Cerere** (Temple of Ceres), the smallest of the three temples, which later served as a Christian church. As you head south, you can pick out the remnants of the Roman city, including an amphitheatre, housing complexes and the **foro** (forum). Beyond lies the **Tempio di Nettuno** (Temple of Neptune), the largest and best preserved of the three temples.

Almost next door, the equally beautiful **basilica** (in reality, a temple to the goddess Hera) is Paestum's oldest surviving monument, dating

LINK YOUR TRIP

3 **Southern Larder**
Join this culinary adventure through Campania where this trip begins – amid the ancient ruins of Paestum – and make your way in reverse order to Sorrento.

DETOUR: PARCO NAZIONALE DEL CILENTO E VALLO DI DIANO

Start: ❶ **Paestum**

Italy's second-largest national park, the **Parco Nazionale del Cilento e Vallo di Diano** (www. cilentoediano.it) occupies the lion's share of the Cilento peninsula. Some of the most interesting and accessible parts lie within an hour's drive northeast of Paestum, in the park's northwest corner. Near the town of **Castelcivita**, you can explore the **Grotte di Castelcivita** (📞0828 77 23 97; www.grottedicastelcivita. com; Piazzale N Zonzi, Castelcivita; adult/reduced €10/8; ⊗standard tours 10.30am, noon, 1.30pm, 3pm, 4.30pm & 6pm Apr-Sep, 10.30am, noon, 1.30pm & 3pm Mar & Oct; 🅿♿), a complex of otherworldly prehistoric caves. For hikers, the town of **Sicignano degli Alburni**, capped by a medieval castle, makes a good base for the tough trek up 1742m-high **Monte Panormo**. Finally, the medieval centre of **Postiglione**, crowned by an 11th-century Norman castle, makes for a lovely stroll.

from the middle of the 6th century BC.

The Drive » Heading 10km south down the SP430 from Paestum, you quickly start winding into the foothills of the Cilento. Agropoli's historic centre will loom up on the right. Follow signs to the 'Centro Storico'.

- - - - - - - - - - - - - - - -

❷ Agropoli (p109)
Guarding the northern flank of the Cilento peninsula, the ancient town of Agropoli proffers stunning views across the Gulf of Salerno to the Amalfi Coast. The outskirts are made up of a rather bland grid of shop-lined streets, but the historic centre,

occupying a rocky promontory, is charming, and features cobbled streets, with ancient churches, the remains of a **castle** and superlative views up and down the coast.

The Drive » South of Agropoli, the 13km stretch of the SR ex SS267 turns inland, giving a taste of Cilento's rugged interior, but you'll quickly head west and to the sea.

- - - - - - - - - - - - - - - -

❸ Santa Maria di Castellabate (p110)
Because of the danger of sudden pirate attacks, all the coastal towns on the Cilento once consisted of a low-lying coastal fishing community and a

nearby highly defended hilltop town where the peasants and fishing families could find quick refuge.

These days, the fishing district of Castellabate – known as Santa Maria di Castellabate – has outgrown its hilltop protector, thanks to the town's 4km beach of golden sand. Despite the development, the town's historic centre preserves a palpable southern-Italian feel, with dusky-pink and ochre houses blinkered by traditional green shutters. The little harbour is especially charming, with its 19th-century *palazzi* (mansions) and the remnants of a much older castle. Note that these charms can diminish quickly when summer crowds overwhelm the scant parking.

The Drive » Just past Santa Maria di Castellabate along the SR ex SS267 is the turnoff to Castellabate. The road then winds through orchards and olive groves for 8km.

PFEIFFER/SHUTTERSTOCK ©

4 Castellabate (p110)

One of the most endearing towns on the Cilento coast, medieval Castellabate clings to the side of a steep hill 280m above sea level. Its summit is marked by the broad **Belvedere di San Costabile**, from where there are sweeping coastal views, and the shell of a 12th-century castle. The surrounding labyrinth of narrow streets is punctuated by ancient archways, small piazzas and the occasional *palazzo*.

The Drive » Head back down to the SR ex SS267 and follow south for 21km. The road leads inland, but you'll see the sea soon enough as you twist down to Acciaroli.

5 Acciaroli (p110)

Despite a growing number of concrete resorts on its outskirts, the tastefully restored historic centre of this fishing village makes it worth a stop, especially

Acciaroli

for Hemingway lovers. The author spent time here in the early 1950s, and some say he based *The Old Man and the Sea* on a local fisherman.

The Drive » After Acciaroli, the coastal highway climbs quickly for 8km to Pioppi, proffering stunning views down the Cilento coast to Capo Palinuro.

6 Pioppi (p110)

A tiny, seaside hamlet, Pioppi enjoys culinary fame as the spiritual home of the Mediterranean diet. For more than 30 years, the American medical researcher Dr Ancel Keys lived here, observing the vigorous residents and studying the health benefits of

their diet. Join the latest generation of locals on lovely Piazza del Millenario, before heading to the pristine, pale pebble beach a few steps away for a picnic.

The Drive » By Cilento standards, it's practically a straight shot for 8km along the coastal highway to the archaeological site of Velia. Some 6km further southeast is Ascea, where coastal mountains make way for the small but rich plains that once fed ancient Velia.

TRIP HIGHLIGHT

7 Velia

Founded by the Greeks in the mid-6th century BC, and subsequently a popular resort for wealthy Romans, Velia (formerly Elea) was once home to philosophers Parmenides and Zeno. Today, you can wander around the town's evocative ruins at the **Parco Archeologico di Elea Velia** (☎0974 97 23 96; Contrada Piana di Velia; adult/reduced €3/1.50; ⊙9am-90min before sunset, Wed-Mon), and explore intact portions of the original city walls, plus remnants of thermal baths, an Ionic temple, a Roman theatre and even a medieval castle.

The Drive 》 You are now headed into the most hair-raising stretch of the Cilento's coastal highway, but spectacular views are your reward. Olive trees start multiplying as you near Pisciotta. The total distance is about 10km.

TRIP HIGHLIGHT

8 Pisciotta (p111)

The liveliest town on the Cilento and also its most dramatic, hilltop Pisciotta consists of a steeply pitched maze of medieval streets. Life centres on the lively main square, Piazza Raffaele Pinto, where the town's largely elderly residents rule the roost. The hills surrounding the town are terraced into rich olive groves and produce particularly prized oil, while local fishermen specialise in anchovies. When their catch is marinated in the local oil, the result is mouthwateringly good.

The Drive 》 The 11km trip begins with a steep descent from Pisciotta, and a straight road to Palinuro. Before reaching town, you'll see its beautiful, miles-long beach.

TRIP HIGHLIGHT

9 Palinuro (p112)

The Cilento's main resort, Palinuro remains remarkably low-key (and low rise), with a tangible fishing-village feel, though its beaches become crowded in August. Extending past its postcard-pretty harbour, the remarkable 2km-long promontory known as **Capo Palinuro** affords wonderful walking trails and views up and down the coast. Better yet, you can visit its sea cliffs and hidden caves, including Palinuro's own version of Capri's famous Grotta Azzurra, with a similarly spectacular display of water, colour and light. **Da Alessandro** (☎347 6540931; www.costieradel cilento.it; Spiaggia del Porto di Palinuro; trips from €15; ⊙mid-Mar–mid-Nov) runs two-hour trips to the grotto and other local caves.

The Drive 》 Begin the 27km drive with a beautiful jaunt along the water before heading inland at Marina di Camerota. Get ready for plenty of sharp turns as you wind up the stunning SR ex SS562.

10 San Giovanni a Piro

With its tight-knit historic centre and jaw-dropping views across the Gulf of Policastro to the mountains of Basilicata and Calabria, this little agricultural town makes a worthy stop as you wind your way around the wild, southern tip of the Cilento peninsula.

The Drive 》 The final 21km of this trip begins with a winding descent from San Giovanni a Piro to the pretty port town of Scario; the road flattens out as you make your way around the picturesque Gulf of Policastro.

11 Sapri

Set on an almost perfectly round natural harbour, Sapri is the ideal place to wave goodbye to the Cilento. The peninsula's dramatic interior mountains rear up across the beautiful Gulf of Policastro. Admire the views from the town's seafront promenade or from one of its nearby beaches.

Right Parco Archeologico di Elea Velia

E55EVU/GETTY IMAGES ©

Destinations

Naples & Pompeii (p54)

Naples explodes with art and antiquities, from colossal Roman statues at Museo Archeologico Nazionale to Caravaggio at Museo di Capodimonte.

Sorrento & Around (p72)

A strangely appealing place, Sorrento oozes laid-back, southern-Italian charm.

Amalfi Coast (p85)

The Amalfi Coast (Costiera Amalfitana) is one of Europe's most breathtaking coasts.

Salerno & the Cilento (p104)

Salerno is an intriguing labyrinth of colourful earthy streets, and the Cilento is home to secluded coves and golden beaches.

Villa Rufolo (p97), Ravello
JEREMY WOODHOUSE/GETTY IMAGES ©

Naples & Pompeii

Blessed with rich volcanic soils, a bountiful sea and centuries of culinary know-how, the Naples region is one of Italy's epicurean heavyweights. Nearby you'll also find Europe's most compelling archaeological site: the ruins of Pompeii.

NAPLES

📞 081 / POP 966,145

Italy's third-largest city is one of its oldest, most artistic and most delicious. Naples' *centro storico* (historic centre) is a Unesco World Heritage Site, its archaeological treasures are among the world's most impressive, and its swag of vain-glorious palaces, castles and churches make Rome look positively provincial.

🔴 Sights

🔵 Centro Storico

⭐ **Museo Archeologico Nazionale**   MUSEUM
(📞848 800288; www.museoarcheologiconapoli.it; Piazza Museo Nazionale 19; adult/reduced €15/2; ⏱9am-7.30pm Wed-Mon; Ⓜ Museo, Piazza Cavour) Naples' National Archaeological Museum serves up one of the world's finest collections

of Graeco-Roman artefacts. The museum was established by the Bourbon king Charles VII in the late 18th century to house the antiquities he inherited from his mother, Elisabetta Farnese, as well as treasures looted from Pompeii and Herculaneum. Star exhibits include the celebrated *Toro Farnese* (Farnese Bull) sculpture and awe-inspiring mosaics from Pompeii's Casa del Fauno (p71).

⭐ **Complesso Monumentale di Santa Chiara**   MONASTERY
(📞081 551 66 73; www.monasterodisantachiara. it; Via Santa Chiara 49c; basilica free, Complesso Monumentale adult/reduced €6/4.50; ⏱basilica 7.30am-1pm & 4.30-8pm, Complesso Monumentale 9.30am-5.30pm Mon-Sat, 10am-2.30pm Sun; Ⓜ Dante) Vast, Gothic and cleverly deceptive, the mighty **Basilica di Santa Chiara** stands at the heart of this tranquil monastery complex. The church was severely damaged in WWII: what you see today is a 20th-century recreation of Gagliardo Primario's 14th-century original. Adjoining it are the basilica's cloisters, adorned with brightly coloured 17th-century majolica tiles and frescoes.

⭐ **Cappella Sansevero**   CHAPEL
(📞081 551 84 70; www.museosansevero.it; Via Francesco de Sanctis 19; adult/reduced €7/5; ⏱9am-7pm Wed-Mon; Ⓜ Dante) It's in this

PLAN YOUR ROUTE

2 **Shadow of Vesuvius** (p27)
Starting in Naples, this trip takes in some of the world's most spectacular ruins in Herculaneum and Pompeii.

Masonic-inspired baroque chapel that you'll find Giuseppe Sanmartino's incredible sculpture, *Cristo velato* (Veiled Christ), its marble veil so realistic that it's tempting to try to lift it and view Christ underneath. It's one of several artistic wonders that include Francesco Queirolo's sculpture *Disinganno* (Disillusion), Antonio Corradini's *Pudicizia* (Modesty) and riotously colourful frescoes by Francesco Maria Russo that have remained untouched since their creation in 1749.

★ Duomo
CATHEDRAL

(☑081 44 90 97; Via Duomo 149; cathedral/baptistry free/€2; ☉cathedral 8.30am-1.30pm & 2.30-7.30pm Mon-Sat, 8.30am-1.30pm & 4.30-7.30pm Sun, baptistry 8.30am-12.30pm & 3.30-6.30pm Mon-Sat, 8.30am-1pm Sun, Cappella di San Gennaro 8.30am-1pm & 3-6.30pm Mon-Sat, 8.30am-1pm & 4.30-7pm Sun; 🚌147,182,184 to Via Foria, Ⓜ Piazza Cavour) Whether you go for Giovanni Lanfranco's fresco in the Cappella di San Gennaro (Chapel of St Janarius), the 4th-century mosaics in the baptistry, or the thrice-annual miracle of San Gennaro, do not miss Naples' cathedral. Kick-started by Charles I of Anjou in 1272 and consecrated in 1315, it was largely destroyed in a 1456 earthquake. It has had copious nips and tucks over the subsequent centuries.

Complesso Monumentale di San Lorenzo Maggiore
ARCHAEOLOGICAL SITE

(☑081 211 08 60; www.laneapolissotterrata.it; Via dei Tribunali 316; church free, museum & excavations guided tour adult/reduced €10/7.50; ☉church 8am-7pm, museum & excavations 9.30am-5.30pm;

Ⓜ Dante) The **basilica** at this richly layered religious complex is deemed one of Naples' finest medieval buildings. Aside from Ferdinando Sanfelice's facade, the Cappella al Rosario and the Cappellone di Sant'Antonio, its baroque makeover was stripped away last century to reveal its austere, Gothic elegance. Beneath the basilica is a sprawl of extraordinary Graeco-Roman **ruins**, accessible on a one-hour guided tour.

Napoli Sotterranea
ARCHAEOLOGICAL SITE

(Underground Naples; ☑081 29 69 44; www.napolisotterranea.org; Piazza San Gaetano 68; adult/reduced €10/8; ☉English tours 10am, noon, 2pm, 4pm & 6pm; Ⓜ Dante) This evocative guided tour leads you 40m below street level to explore Naples' ancient labyrinth of aqueducts, passages and cisterns.

The passages were originally hewn by the Greeks to extract tufa stone used in construction and to channel water from Mt Vesuvius. Extended by the Romans, the network of conduits and cisterns was more recently used as an air-raid shelter in WWII. Part of the tour takes place by candlelight via extremely narrow passages – not suitable for expanded girths!

Pio Monte della Misericordia
CHURCH, MUSEUM

(☑081 44 69 44; www.piomontedellamisericordia.it; Via dei Tribunali 253; adult/reduced €7/5; ☉9am-6pm Mon-Sat, to 2.30pm Sun; Ⓜ Piazza Cavour) The 1st-floor gallery of this octagonal, 17th-century church delivers a satisfying, digestible collection of Renaissance and baroque art, including works by Francesco

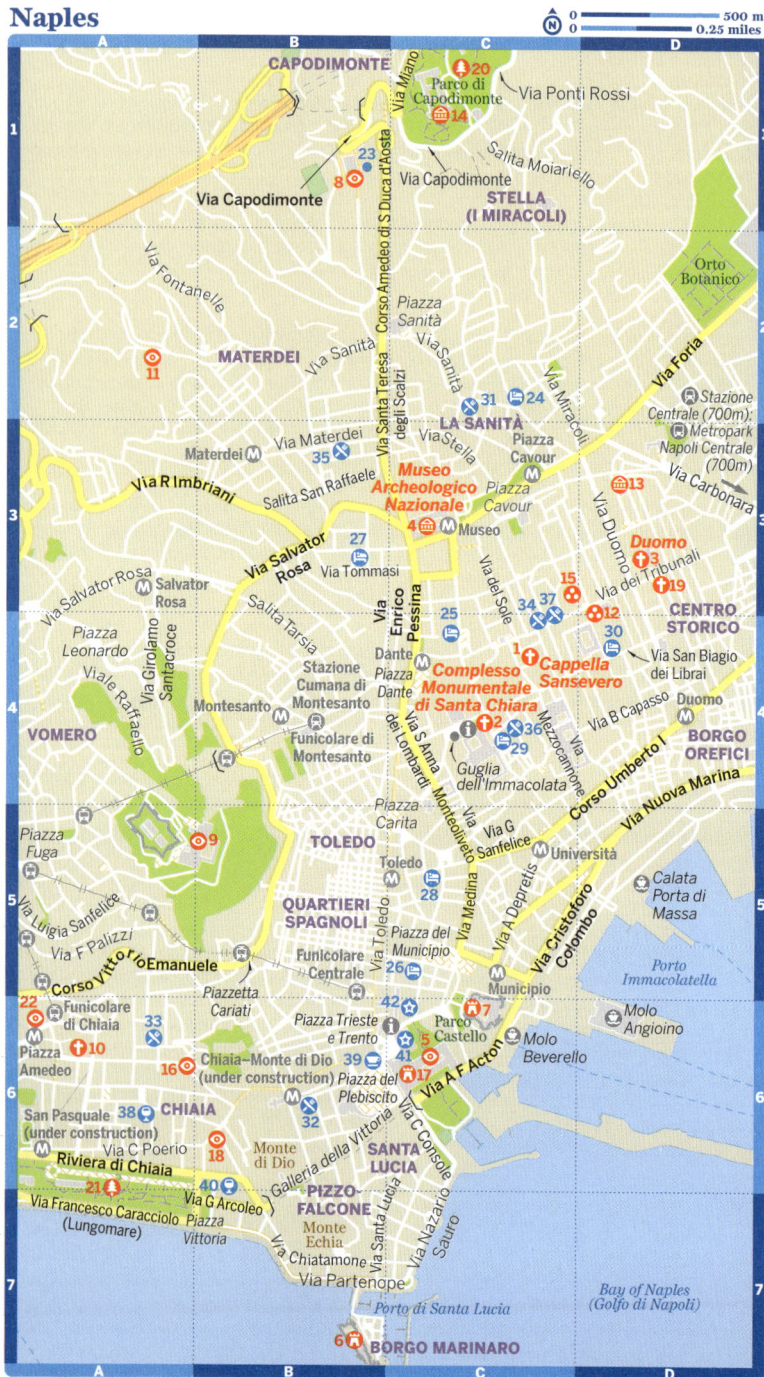

Naples

0 — 500 m
0 — 0.25 miles

CAPODIMONTE

Via Milano

20
Parco di
Capodimonte · Via Ponti Rossi
14

23
8
Via Capodimonte

Salita Moiariello

Via Capodimonte

STELLA
(I MIRACOLI)

Orto
Botanico

Corso Amedeo di S Duca d'Aosta

Via Fontanelle

Piazza
Sanità

MATERDEI

11

Via Sanità

Via Sanità

Via Santa Teresa degli Scalzi

Via Foria

Stazione
Centrale (700m);
Metropark
Napoli Centrale
(700m)

LA SANITÀ

31 24

Via Stella

Via Miracoli

Piazza
Cavour

Via Carbonara

Via Materdei

Materdei

35

Museo
Archeologico
Nazionale

Piazza
Cavour

13

Via R Imbriani

Salita San Raffaele

4 Museo

Via Duomo

Duomo

3

Via Salvator
Rosa

27

Via Tommasi

Via del Sole

15

Via dei Tribunali

19

Via Salvator Rosa

Salvator
Rosa

Salita Tarsia

Via Enrico Pessina

25

34 37

12

30

CENTRO
STORICO

Piazza
Leonardo

Via Girolamo Santacroce

Viale Raffaello

Dante

Piazza
Dante

1

Cappella
Sansevero

Via San Biagio
dei Librai

Montesanto

Stazione
Cumana di
Montesanto

Complesso
Monumentale
di Santa Chiara

Via B Capasso

Duomo

BORGO
OREFICI

Funicolare di
Montesanto

36

2

VOMERO

Via S Anna
di Lombardi

29

Via Mezzocannone

Corso Umberto I

Via Nuova Marina

Guglia
dell'Immacolata

9

Piazza
Carita

TOLEDO

Via G
Sanfelice

Università

Calata
Porta di
Massa

Piazza
Fuga

Toledo

28

Via Medina

Via A Depretis

Via Cristoforo Colombo

Porto
Immacolatella

Via Luigia Sanfelice

Via F Palizzi

QUARTIERI
SPAGNOLI

Via Toledo

Piazza del
Municipio

Molo
Angioino

Corso Vittorio Emanuele

Funicolare
Centrale

26

Municipio

22

Funicolare
di Chiaia

33

42

Piazzetta
Cariati

Piazza Trieste
e Trento

5

Parco
Castello

7

Molo
Beverello

Piazza
Amedeo

10

16

Chiaia–Monte di Dio
(under construction)

39

41

17

Via A F Acton

38

CHIAIA

32

San Pasquale
(under construction)

Piazza del
Plebiscito

Via C Poerio

18

Monte
di Dio

Riviera di Chiaia

40

Galleria della Vittoria

SANTA
LUCIA

21

Via G Arcoleo

PIZZO-
FALCONE

Via Console

Via Francesco Caracciolo
(Lungomare)

Piazza
Vittoria

Monte
Echia

Via Santa Lucia

Via Nazario Sauro

Chiatamone

Via Partenope

Bay of Naples
(Golfo di Napoli)

Porto di Santa Lucia

6

BORGO MARINARO

Naples

de Mura, Jusepe de Ribera, Andrea Vaccaro and Paul van Somer. It's also home to contemporary artworks by Italian and foreign artists, each inspired by Caravaggio's masterpiece *Le sette opere di Misericordia* (The Seven Acts of Mercy). Considered by many to be the most important painting in Naples, you'll find it above the main altar in the ground-floor chapel.

MADRE
GALLERY

(Museo d'Arte Contemporanea Donnaregina; ☑ 081 1973 7254; www.madrenapoli.it; Via Settembrini 79; adult/reduced €8/4; ⊙ 10am-7.30pm Mon & Wed-Sat, to 8pm Sun; Ⓜ Piazza Cavour) When *Madonna and Child* overload hits, reboot at Naples' museum of modern and contemporary art. In the lobby, French conceptual artist Daniel Buren sets the mood with his playful, mirror-panelled installation *Work in Situ,* with other specially commissioned installations from heavyweights like Anish Kapoor, Rebecca Horn and Sol LeWitt on level one. Level two houses the bulk of MADRE's permanent collection of painting, sculpture and photography from other prolific 20th- and 21st-century artists.

◉ Vomero

Certosa e Museo di San Martino
MONASTERY, MUSEUM

(☑ 081 229 45 03; www.polomusealecampania. beniculturali.it/index.php/certosa-e-museo; Largo San Martino 5; adult/reduced €6/3; ⊙ 8.30am-7.30pm Tue & Thu-Sat, to 6.30pm Sun; Ⓜ Vanvitelli, ▣ Montesanto to Morghen) The high point (quite literally) of the Neapolitan baroque, this charterhouse-turned-museum was built as a Carthusian monastery between 1325 and 1368. Centred on one of the most beautiful cloisters in Italy, it has been decorated, adorned and altered over the centuries by some of Italy's finest talent, most importantly architect Giovanni Antonio Dosio in the 16th century and baroque sculptor Cosimo Fanzago a century later. Nowadays, it's a superb repository of Neapolitan and Italian artistry.

The monastery's **church** and the sacristy, treasury and chapter house that flank it contain a feast of frescoes and paintings by some of Naples' greatest 17th-century artists, among them Battista Caracciolo, Jusepe de Ribera, Guido Reni and Massimo Stanzione.

In the nave, Cosimo Fanzago's inlaid marble work is simply extraordinary.

It's worth noting that some sections of the museum are only open at various times of the day; see the website for specific times.

◉ Santa Lucia & Chiaia

Palazzo Reale   PALACE

(Royal Palace; ☑ 081 40 05 47; www.coopculture.it; Piazza del Plebiscito 1; adult/reduced €6/3; ⊙9am-8pm Thu-Tue; ☐ R2 to Via San Carlo, Ⓜ Municipio) Envisaged as a 16th-century monument to Spanish glory (Naples was under Spanish rule at the time), the magnificent Palazzo Reale is home to the **Museo del Palazzo Reale**, a rich and eclectic collection of baroque and neoclassical furnishings, porcelain, tapestries, sculpture and paintings, spread across the palace's royal apartments.

Among the many highlights is the **Teatrino di Corte**, a lavish private theatre created by Ferdinando Fuga in 1768 to celebrate the marriage of Ferdinand IV and Marie Caroline of Austria. Incredibly, Angelo Viva's statues of Apollo and the Muses set along the walls are made of papier mâché.

The **Cappella Reale** (Royal Chapel) houses an 18th-century *presepe napoletano* (Neapolitan nativity scene). Fastidiously detailed, its cast of *pastori* (nativity-scene figurines) were crafted by a series of celebrated Neapolitan artists, including Giuseppe Sanmartino, creator of the *Cristo velato* (Veiled Christ) sculpture in the Cappella Sansevero.

The palace is also home to the **Biblioteca Nazionale di Napoli** (National Library; ☑ 081 781 91 11; www.bnnonline.it; ⊙8.30am-7pm Mon-Fri, to 1.30pm Sat, papyri exhibition by appointment only, Sezione Lucchesi Palli 8.30am-6.45pm Mon-Thu, to 3.30pm Fri) **FREE**, its own priceless treasures including at least 2000 papyri discovered at Herculaneum. Bring photo ID to enter the Biblioteca Nazionale.

Castel Nuovo   CASTLE

(☑ 081 795 77 22; Piazza Municipio; adult/reduced €6/3; ⊙8.30am-6pm Mon-Sat, 10am-1pm Sun; Ⓜ Municipio) Locals know this 13th-century castle as the Maschio Angioino (Angevin Keep), and its Cappella Palatina is home to fragments of frescoes by Giotto; they're on the splays of the Gothic windows. You'll also find Roman ruins under the glass-floored Sala dell'Armeria (Armoury Hall). The castle's upper floors (closed on Sunday) house a collection of mostly 17th- to early-20th-century Neapolitan paintings. The top floor houses the more interesting works, including landscape paintings by Luigi Crisconio and a watercolour by architect Carlo Vanvitelli.

◉ Capodimonte & La Sanità

Museo di Capodimonte   MUSEUM

(☑ 081 749 91 11; www.museocapodimonte.beni culturali.it; Via Miano 2; adult/reduced €12/8; ⊙8.30am-7.30pm Thu-Tue; ☐ R4, 178 to Via Capodimonte, ☐ Shuttle Capodimonte) Southern Italy's largest and richest art gallery, its vast collection – much of which Charles inherited from his mother, Elisabetta Farnese – was moved here in 1759 and ranges from exquisite 12th-century altarpieces to works by Botticelli, Caravaggio, Titian and Warhol.

The gallery is spread over three floors and 160 rooms; for most people, a full morning or afternoon is enough for an abridged best-of tour. The 1st floor includes works by greats such as Michelangelo, Raphael and Titian, with highlights including Masaccio's *Crocifissione* (Crucifixion), Botticelli's *Madonna col bambino e due angeli* (Madonna with Child and Angels), Bellini's *Trasfigurazione* (Transfiguration) and Parmigianino's *Antea*, all of which are subject to room changes within the museum.

The floor is also home to the royal apartments, a study in regal excess. The **Salottino di Porcellana** (Room 52) is an outrageous

---

ⓘ BEFORE YOU EXPLORE

If you're planning to blitz the sights, the **Campania Artecard** (☑ 800 600601; www.campaniaartecard.it) is an excellent investment. A cumulative ticket that covers museum admission and transport, it comes in various forms.

The Naples three-day ticket (adult/reduced €21/12) gives free admission to three participating sites, up to 50% off on others and free use of public transport in the city.

Other handy options include a seven-day 'Tutta la Regione' ticket (€34), which offers free admission to five sites and discounted admission to others in areas as far afield as Caserta, Ravello (Amalfi Coast) and Paestum. The latter does not cover transport.

Cards can be purchased online or at participating sites and museums.

Cimitero delle Fontanelle

example of 18th-century chinoiserie, its walls and ceiling dense with whimsically themed porcelain 'stucco'. Originally created between 1757 and 1759 for the Palazzo Reale in Portici, it was transferred to Capodimonte in 1867.

Upstairs, the 2nd-floor galleries display work by Neapolitan artists from the 13th to the 19th centuries, including de Ribera, Giordano, Solimena and Stanzione. It's also home to some spectacular 16th-century Belgian tapestries. The piece that many come to see, however, is Caravaggio's *Flagellazione* (Flagellation of Christ; 1607–10), which hangs in reverential solitude in Room 78. Rooms 88 to 95 are dedicated to paintings of the Neapolitan baroque period.

Accessed from the 2nd floor, a small mezzanine level hosts a rotating selection of modern works from artists including Andy Warhol, Mimmo Jodice and John Armleder.

Once you've finished in the museum, the **Real Bosco di Capodimonte** (www.boscodicapodimonte.it; ⊙ 7am-7.30pm Apr-Sep, to 6pm Feb, Mar & Oct, to 5pm Nov-Jan) **FREE** – the palace's 134-hectare estate – provides a much-needed breath of fresh air.

Catacombe di San Gennaro   CATACOMB
(☑ 081 744 37 14; www.catacombedinapoli.it; Via Capodimonte 13; adult/reduced €9/6; ⊙ 1hr tours hourly 10am-5pm Mon-Sat, to 2pm Sun; 🚍 R4, 178 to Via Capodimonte) Naples' oldest and most sacred catacombs became a Christian pilgrimage site when San Gennaro's body was interred here in the 5th century. The

carefully restored site allows visitors to experience an evocative other world of tombs, corridors and broad vestibules, its treasures including 2nd-century Christian frescoes, 5th-century mosaics and the oldest known portrait of San Gennaro, dating from the second half of the 5th century.

Cimitero delle Fontanelle   CEMETERY
(☑ 081 1925 6964; www.cimiterofontanelle.com; Via Fontanelle 80; ⊙ 10am-5pm; 🚍 C51 to Via Fontanelle, Ⓜ Materdei) **FREE** Holding about eight million human bones, the ghoulish Fontanelle Cemetery was first used during the 1656 plague, before becoming Naples' main burial site during the 1837 cholera epidemic. At the end of the 19th century it became a hot spot for the *anime pezzentelle* (poor souls) cult, in which locals adopted skulls and prayed for their souls. Lack of information at the site makes joining a tour much more rewarding; reputable outfits include **Cooperativa Sociale Onlus 'La Paranza'** (☑ 081 744 37 14; www.catacombedinapoli.it; Via Capodimonte 13; ⊙ information point 10am-5pm Mon-Sat, to 2pm Sun; 🚍 R4, 178 to Via Capodimonte).

🎉 Festivals & Events

Maggio dei Monumenti   CULTURAL
(www.comune.napoli.it; ⊙ May) A month-long cultural feast, with a bounty of concerts, performances, exhibitions, guided tours and other events across Naples. The festival program is usually released on the Comune di Napoli (Naples City Council) website.

City Walk
An Architectural Saunter

START PIAZZA AMEDEO
END CASTEL DELL'OVO
LENGTH 2.2KM; 1.5 HOURS

Begin the walk outside Piazza Amedeo metro station on **1 Piazza Amedeo**. Just off its northern end stands former hotel **2 Villa Maria** (Via del Parco Margherita 1), one of Naples' finest examples of art nouveau architecture. From the southeast side of Piazza Amedeo, slip into Via Vittorio Colonna (which becomes Via dei Mille). To your left you'll pass the unapologetically baroque **3 Chiesa di Santa Teresa a Chiaia** (☎ 081 41 42 63; Via Vittorio Colonna 22; ⊙ 7.30-11am Mon-Sat, 8.30am-noon & 5-7.30pm Sun), designed by Cosimo Fanzago and home to paintings by Luca Giordano.

Via dei Mille eventually kinks southeast, becoming Via Filangieri. It's here that you'll find art nouveau **4 Palazzo Mannajuolo** (Via Filangieri 36; ⊙ 8am-9pm). Wander inside to admire its spiral staircase, famously featured in *Napoli velata* (Naples in Veils), a

film by prolific Turkish-Italian director Ferzan Özpetek. Continue along Via Filangieri, then turn right into Via Santa Caterina. The street leads to dashing **5 Piazza dei Martiri**, its 19th-century centrepiece dedicated to Neapolitan martyrs. The monument's four lions represent the anti-Bourbon uprisings of 1799, 1820, 1848 and 1860. At No 30 is Palazzo Calabritto, designed by architect Luigi Vanvitelli, most famous for his monumental Reggia di Caserta.

Head south on exclusive Via Calabritto, cross busy Piazza Vittoria – which flanks former Bourbon garden **6 Villa Comunale** (Piazza Vittoria; ⊙ 7am-midnight) – and turn left into Via Partenope (Lungomare), a pedestrianised seafront promenade popular with everyone from love-struck teens to boisterous families. The strip leads to Via Eldorado and the ancient islet of Borgo Marinaro, home to the **7 Castel dell'Ovo** (☎ 081 795 45 92; Borgo Marinaro; ⊙ 9am-7.30pm Mon-Sat, to 2pm Sun Apr-Oct, reduced hours Nov-Mar) FREE and its silver screen–worthy rooftop views.

★Napoli Teatro Festival Italia THEATRE

(www.napoliteatrofestival.it; ☉ Jun/Jul) One month of local and international theatre, dance and performance art, staged in conventional and unconventional venues.

🛏 Sleeping

Where to slumber? The *centro storico* is studded with important churches and sights, artisan studios and student-packed bars. Seafront Santa Lucia delivers grand hotels, while sceney Chiaia is best for fashionable shops and *aperitivo* (aperitif) bars. The lively, laundry-strung Quartieri Spagnoli is within walking distance of all three neighbourhoods.

★The Church B&B €

(✆081 1952 9272; www.thechurch.it; Via San Biagio dei Librai 39; d €50-100, tr €70-130; ❄🛜; 🚇R2 to Corso Umberto I) On the 4th floor of an anecdote-rich 16th-century *palazzo*, this intimate, cultured B&B is decorated with contemporary Neapolitan photography and cleverly upcycled objects, from coffee percolators turned plant pots to an African tek tree turned bookshelf. The four minimalist rooms are equally whimsical; the top-floor room is the most coveted and comes with a striking in-room shower and private terrace.

★Magma Home B&B €

(✆320 4360272, 338 3188914; http://magmahome.it; Via San Giuseppe dei Nudi 18; d €70-150; ❄🛜; Ⓜ Museo) 🌿 Contemporary artworks, cultural soirées and impeccable hospitality plug you straight into Naples' cultural scene at Magma. Its eight rooms – each designed by a local artist – intrigue with their mix of Italian design classics, upcycled materials and specially commissioned artworks. There's a large, contemporary communal kitchen and living area, plus two inviting rooftop terraces with views of the city and Mt Vesuvius.

★Schiara B&B €

(✆081 033 09 77, 338 9264453; www.maisons decharme.it; Vico Volpicelli 20; s €30-85, d €50-100, tr €65-110, q €80-125; ❄@🛜; Ⓜ Dante) Freshly minted B&B Schiara offers five contemporary rooms, each with en-suite bathroom and playful artisan details inspired by southern-Italian themes. The 'Miti' room comes with its own in-room soaking tub, while the upstairs 'Riti' room has a kitchenette and private rooftop terrace. All guests have access to a gorgeous outdoor terrace and communal rooftop garden with sunbeds and bewitching views.

Neapolitan Trips HOSTEL €

(✆B&B 081 551 8977, hostel 081 1836 6402, hotel 081 1984 5933; www.neapolitantrips.com; Via dei Fiorentini 10; hostel dm €15-35, B&B d €45-90, hotel d €80-160; ❄🛜; Ⓜ Toledo) Neapolitan Trips is a unique beast, with a clean, next-gen hostel on one floor, and both B&B and hotel rooms on another. The hostel is the standout, boasting a hip communal lounge-bar complete with electric guitars, amps and a piano for impromptu evening jams, a modern guest kitchen with complimentary pasta to cook, and mixed-gender dorms with USB ports by each bed.

★Atelier Inès B&B €€

(✆349 4433422; www.atelierinesgallery.com; Via dei Cristallini 138; d €135-170; ❄🛜; 🚌C51, C52 to Via dei Vergini, Ⓜ Piazza Cavour) A stylish, eclectic oasis in the earthy Sanità district, this three-suite B&B is a homage to the late Neapolitan sculptor and designer Annibale Oste, whose **workshop** (www.annibaleoste.com/esperienza -oste/; ☉ usually 9am-6pm Mon-Fri) shares a leafy courtyard. Everything from the lamps and spiral towel racks to the one-of-a-kind sculptural bedheads are Oste's whimsical designs, complemented by heavenly mattresses, a choice of pillows, and Vietri-ceramic bathrooms with satisfyingly hot water.

★Hotel Piazza Bellini BOUTIQUE HOTEL €€

(✆081 45 17 32; www.hotelpiazzabellini.com; Via Santa Maria di Costantinopoli 101; d €90-190; ❄@🛜; Ⓜ Dante) Only steps from the bars and nightlife of Piazza Bellini, this sharp, hip hotel occupies a 16th-century *palazzo*, its pure-white spaces spiked with original majolica tiles, vaulted ceilings and *piperno*-stone paving. Rooms are modern and functional, with designer fittings, fluffy duvets and chic bathrooms with excellent showers. Four rooms on the 5th and 6th floors feature panoramic terraces.

★La Ciliegina Lifestyle Hotel BOUTIQUE HOTEL €€€

(✆081 1971 8800; www.cilieginahotel.it; Via PE Imbriani 30; d from €200; ❄@🛜; Ⓜ Municipio) An easy walk from the hydrofoil terminal, this chic, contemporary slumber spot is a hit with fashion-conscious urbanites. Spacious white rooms are splashed with blue and red accents, each with top-of-the-range Hästens beds, flat-screen TVs and marble-clad bathrooms with a water-jet jacuzzi shower (one junior suite has a jacuzzi tub).

Teatro San Carlo

✕ Eating

Naples is one of Italy's gastronomic darlings, and the bonus of a bayside setting makes for some seriously memorable meals. While white linen, candlelight and €50 bills are readily available, some of the best bites await in the city's spit-and-sawdust trattorias, where two courses can cost under €20.

★ Concettina Ai Tre Santi   PIZZA €

(☑ 081 29 00 37; www.pizzeriaoliva.it; Via Arena della Sanità 7; pizzas from €5; ⊙ noon-midnight Mon-Sat, to 5pm Sun; 🕿; Ⓜ Piazza Cavour, Museo) Head in by noon (or 7.30pm at dinner) to avoid a long wait at this hot-spot pizzeria, made famous thanks to its young, driven *pizzaiolo* Ciro Oliva. The menu is an index of fastidiously sourced artisanal ingredients, used to top Ciro's flawless, wood-fired bases. Traditional Neapolitan pizza aside, you'll also find a string of creative seasonal options.

★ Pizzeria Starita   PIZZA €

(☑ 081 557 36 82; www.pizzeriestarita.it; Via Materdei 28; pizzas from €4; ⊙ noon-3.30pm & 7pm-midnight Tue-Sun; Ⓜ Materdei) The giant fork and ladle hanging on the wall at this historic pizzeria were used by Sophia Loren in *L'oro di Napoli,* and the kitchen made the *pizze fritte* sold by the actress in the film. While the 60-plus pizza varieties include a tasty *fiorilli e zucchine* (zucchini, zucchini flowers and *provola*), our allegiance remains to its classic marinara.

Serafino   SICILIAN €

(☑ 081 557 14 33; Via dei Tribunali 44; arancini, cannoli €2.50; ⊙ 10.30am-10.30pm Mon-Thu, to midnight Fri-Sun) A veritable porthole to Sicily, this takeaway stand peddles authentic island street food. Savoury bites include various types of *arancini* (deep-fried rice balls), among them *al ragù* (with meat sauce) and *alla Norma* (with fried aubergine and ricotta). The real reason to head here, however, is for the crisp, flawless cannoli, filled fresh with silky Sicilian ricotta and sprinkled with pistachio crumbs. Bliss.

Pizzeria Gino Sorbillo   PIZZA €

(☑ 081 44 66 43; www.sorbillo.it; Via dei Tribunali 32; pizzas from €4; ⊙ noon-3.30pm & 7-11.30pm Mon-Sat; 🕿; Ⓜ Dante) Day in, day out, this cult-status pizzeria is besieged by hungry hordes. While debate may rage over whether Gino Sorbillo's pizzas are the best in town, there's no doubt that his giant, wood-fired discs – made using organic flour and tomatoes – will have you licking fingertips and whiskers. Head in early.

★ Da Ettore   NEAPOLITAN €€

(☑ 081 764 35 78; Via Gennaro Serra 39; meals €25; ⊙ 1-3pm & 8-10pm Tue-Sat, 1-3pm Sun; 🕿; 🚍 R2 to Via San Carlo, Ⓜ Chiaia-Monte di Dio) This homey, eight-table trattoria has an epic reputation. Scan the walls for famous fans like comedy great Totò, and a framed passage from crime writer Massimo Siviero, who mentions Ettore in one of his tales. The draw is solid regional cooking, which includes one of the best *spaghetti alle vongole* (spaghetti with clams) in town. Book two days ahead for Sunday lunch.

★ Salumeria
NEAPOLITAN €€

(☏ 081 1936 4649; www.salumeriaupnea.it; Via San Giovanni Maggiore Pignatelli 34/35; sandwiches from €5.50, charcuterie platters from €8.50, meals around €30; ⏱ 12.30-5pm & 7.15pm-midnight Thu-Tue; 🖥; M Dante) Small producers, local ingredients and contemporary takes on provincial Campanian recipes drive bistro-inspired Salumeria. Nibble on quality charcuterie and cheeses or fill up on artisanal *panini*, hamburgers or Salumeria's sublime *ragù napoletano* (pasta served in a rich tomato-and-meat sauce slow-cooked over two days). Even the ketchup here is made in-house, using DOP Piennolo tomatoes from Vesuvius.

★ L'Ebbrezza di Noè
ITALIAN €€

(☏ 081 40 01 04; www.lebbrezzadinoe.com; Vico Vetriera 9; meals €35-40, cheese & charcuterie platters €10; ⏱ 6-11pm Tue-Thu, to midnight Fri & Sat, 1-3pm Sun; 🖥; M Piazza Amedeo) A wine shop by day, 'Noah's Drunkenness' transforms into an intimate culinary hot spot by night. Slip inside for vino and conversation with sommelier Luca at the bar, or settle into one of the bottle-lined dining rooms for seductive, market-driven dishes such as house special *paccheri fritti* (fried pasta stuffed with aubergine and served with fresh basil and a rich tomato sauce).

Drinking & Nightlife

Although Neapolitans aren't big drinkers, Naples offers an increasingly varied selection of venues in which to imbibe. You'll find well-worn wine bars and a new wave of options focused on craft beer, cocktails and even speciality coffee. The main hubs are the *centro storico* and Chiaia. The former is generally cheaper and more alternative, the latter more fashionable and scene-y.

★ L'Antiquario
COCKTAIL BAR

(☏ 081 764 53 90; www.facebook.com/Antiquario Napoli; Via Gaetani 2; ⏱ 7.30pm-2.30am; 🚍 151, 154 to Piazza Vittoria) If you take your cocktails seriously, slip into this sultry, speakeasy-inspired den. Wrapped in art nouveau wallpaper, it's the domain of Neapolitan barkeep Alex Frezza, a finalist at the 2014 Bombay Sapphire World's Most Imaginative Bartender Awards. Straddling classic and contemporary, the drinks are impeccable, made with passion and meticulous attention to detail.

★ Barril
BAR

(☏ 393 9814362; www.barril.it; Via G Fiorelli 11; ⏱ 7pm-2am Tue-Thu & Sun, to 3am Fri & Sat; 🖥; M Piazza Amedeo) From street level, stairs lead down to this softly lit, buzzing garden bar, where grown-up, fashionable types mingle among birdcage seats and vintage Cinzano posters. Fresh, competent cocktails include giant, creamy piña coladas, and you'll also find over 40 gins with numerous tonic waters for a customised G&T.

★ Caffè Gambrinus
CAFE

(☏ 081 41 75 82; www.grancaffegambrinus.com; Via Chiaia 1-2; ⏱ 7am-1am Sun-Fri, to 2am Sat; 🚍 R2 to Via San Carlo, M Municipio) Gambrinus is Naples' oldest and most venerable cafe, serving superlative Neapolitan coffee under flouncy chandeliers. Oscar Wilde knocked back a few here and Mussolini had some rooms shut to keep out left-wing intellectuals. Sit-down prices are steep, but the *aperitivo* nibbles are decent and sipping a *spritz* or a luscious *cioccolata calda* (hot chocolate) in its belle-époque rooms is something worth savouring.

☆ Entertainment

Although Naples is no London or Milan on the entertainment front, it does offer world-class opera, ballet, classical music and jazz, thought-provoking theatre and in-the-know DJs. To see what's on, scan Italian-language *Corriere del Mezzogiorno* (https://corriere delmezzogiorno.corriere.it/napoli) or *La Repubblica* (http://napoli.repubblica.it), or ask at the tourist office.

★ Teatro San Carlo
OPERA, BALLET

(☏ box office 081 797 23 31; www.teatrosancarlo.it; Via San Carlo 98; ⏱ box office 10am-9pm Mon-Sat, to 6pm Sun; 🚍 R2 to Via San Carlo, M Municipio) San Carlo's opera season runs from November or December to June, with occasional summer performances. Sample prices: a place in the 6th tier (from €35), the stalls (€75 to €130) or the side box (from €40). Ballet season runs from late October to April or early May; tickets range from €30 to €110.

★ Stadio San Paolo
FOOTBALL

(Piazzale Vincenzo Tecchio; M Napoli Campi Flegrei) Naples' football team, Napoli, is the fourth most supported in Italy, and watching it play in the country's third-largest stadium is a rush. The season runs from late August to late May; seats cost from around €20 to €100; bring photo ID.

Information

MEDICAL SERVICES

Loreto Mare Hospital (Ospedale San Maria di Loreto Nuovo; ☑ 081 254 21 11; www.aslnapoli 1centro.it/818; Via Vespucci 26; ☐ 154 to Via Vespucci) Central-city hospital with an emergency department.

Pharmacy (Napoli Centrale; ⊙ 7am-9.30pm Mon-Sat (to 9pm in winter), 8am-9pm Sun; Ⓜ Garibaldi, Ⓡ Napoli Centrale) Pharmacy inside the main train station.

TOURIST INFORMATION

Tourist Information Office (☑ 081 551 27 01; www.inaples.it; Piazza del Gesù Nuovo 7; ⊙ 9am-5pm Mon-Sat, to 1pm Sun; Ⓜ Dante) In the *centro storico*.

Tourist Information Office (☑ 081 40 23 94; www.inaples.it; Via San Carlo 9; ⊙ 9am-5pm Mon-Sat, to 1pm Sun; Ⓡ R2 to Via San Carlo, Ⓜ Municipio) At Galleria Umberto I, directly opposite Teatro San Carlo.

Getting There & Away

AIR

Naples International Airport (Capodichino) (☑ 081 789 62 59; www.aeroportodinapoli. it; Viale F Ruffo di Calabria), 7km northeast of the city centre, is southern Italy's main airport. It's served by a number of major airlines and low-cost carriers, including easyJet, which operates flights to Naples from London, Paris, Amsterdam, Vienna, Berlin and several other European cities.

CAR & MOTORCYCLE

Naples is on the north–south Autostrada del Sole, the A1 (north to Rome and Milan) and the A3 (south to Salerno and Reggio di Calabria).

Ⓘ Getting Around

TO/FROM THE AIRPORT

Alibus airport buses (€5) run to Napoli Centrale (Piazza Garibaldi) and the main cruise-ship and ferry terminals. Buses run from 6am to 11.30pm. Set taxi fares are €18 to Napoli Centrale (Piazza Garibaldi) and the *centro storico*, €21 to Piazza Municipio or the Molo Beverello fast-ferry and hydrofoil terminal, and €25 to Chiaia, Mergellina and Posillipo.

CAR & MOTORCYCLE

Vehicle theft, anarchic traffic and illegal parking 'attendants' make driving in Naples a bad option. Furthermore, much of the city centre is closed to nonresident traffic for much of the day.

Vespa Sprint (☑ 081 764 34 52; Via Santa Lucia 36; scooter hire per day from €60; ⊙ 8am-8pm Mon-Sat, 10am-6pm Sun)

SOUTH OF NAPLES

Herculaneum (Ercolano)

Ercolano is an uninspiring Neapolitan suburb that's home to one of Italy's best-preserved ancient sites: Herculaneum. A superbly conserved fishing town, the site is smaller and less daunting than Pompeii, allowing you to visit without the nagging feeling that you're bound to miss something.

Sights

★ Ruins of Herculaneum
ARCHAEOLOGICAL SITE

(☑ 081 777 70 08; http://ercolano.beniculturali.it; Corso Resina 187, Ercolano; adult/reduced €13/2; ⊙ 8.30am-7.30pm, last entry 6pm Apr-Oct, 8.30am-5pm, last entry 3.30pm Nov-Mar; Ⓟ; Ⓡ Circumvesuviana to Ercolano–Scavi) Herculaneum harbours a wealth of archaeological finds, from ancient advertisements and stylish mosaics to carbonised furniture and terror-struck skeletons. Indeed, this superbly conserved Roman fishing town of 4000 inhabitants is easier to navigate than Pompeii, and can be explored with a map and highly recommended audio guide (€8).

To reach the ruins from Ercolano–Scavi train station, walk downhill to the very end of Via IV Novembre and through the archway across the street. The path leads down to the ticket office, which lies on your left. Ticket purchased, follow the walkway around to the actual entrance to the ruins, where you can also hire audio guides.

Herculaneum's fate runs parallel to that of Pompeii. Destroyed by an earthquake in AD 62, the AD 79 eruption of Mt Vesuvius saw it submerged in a 16m-thick sea of mud that essentially fossilised the city. This meant that even delicate items, such as furniture and clothing, were discovered remarkably well preserved. Tragically, the inhabitants didn't fare so well; thousands of people tried to escape by boat but were suffocated by the volcano's poisonous gases. Indeed, what appears to be a moat around the town is in fact the ancient shoreline. It was here in 1980 that archaeologists discovered some 300 skeletons, the remains of a crowd that had fled to the beach only to be overcome by the terrible heat of clouds surging down from Vesuvius.

The town itself was rediscovered in 1709 and amateur excavations were carried out

Ruins of Herculaneum

intermittently until 1874, with many finds carted off to Naples to decorate the houses of the well-to-do or ending up in museums. Serious archaeological work began again in 1927 and continues to this day; with much of the ancient site buried beneath modern Ercolano, it's slow going.

Terme Suburbane ARCHAEOLOGICAL SITE

(Suburban Baths) Marking Herculaneum's southernmost tip is the 1st-century-AD Terme Suburbane, one of the best-preserved Roman bath complexes in existence, with deep pools, stucco friezes and bas-reliefs looking down upon marble seats and floors. This is also one of the best places to observe the soaring volcanic deposits that smothered the ancient coastline.

MAV MUSEUM

(Museo Archeologico Virtuale; ☑ 081 777 68 43; www.museomav.com; Via IV Novembre 44; adult/reduced €10/8; ⊙ 9am-5.30pm daily Mar-May, 10am-6.30pm daily Jun-Sep, to 4pm Tue-Sun Oct-Feb; 🚻; 🚇 Circumvesuviana to Ercolano–Scavi) Using computer-generated recreations, this 'virtual archaeological museum' brings ruins such as Pompeii's forum and Capri's Villa Jovis back to virtual life. Some of the displays are in Italian only. The short documentary gives an overview of the history of Mt Vesuvius and its infamous eruption in AD 79... in rather lacklustre 3D. The museum is on the main street linking Ercolano–Scavi train station to the ruins of Herculaneum.

✗ Eating

Viva Lo Re NEAPOLITAN €€

(☑ 081 739 02 07; www.vivalore.it; Corso Resina 261, Ercolano; meals €32; ⊙ noon-3.30pm & 7.30-11.30pm Tue-Sat, noon-3.30pm Sun; 🛜) Whether you're after an inspired meal or a simple glass of vino, this refined yet relaxed *osteria* (casual tavern) is a solid choice. The wine list is extensive and impressive, while the menu offers competent, produce-driven regional cooking with subtle modern twists. For an appetite-piquing overview, start with the multitaste *antipasto Viva Lo Re*.

The *osteria* lies 500m southeast of the Herculaneum ruins on Corso Resina, dubbed the *Miglio d'Oro* (Golden Mile) for its once glorious stretch of 18th-century villas.

ℹ Information

Tourist Office (☑ 081 788 13 75; Via IV Novembre 44; ⊙ 9am-2pm Mon-Fri & 2.30-5pm Tue & Thu; 🚇 Circumvesuviana to Ercolano–Scavi) Ercolano's tourist office is in the same building as MAV, between the Circumvesuviana Ercolano–Scavi train station and the Herculaneum *scavi* (ruins).

ℹ Getting There & Away

If driving from Naples, the SS18 runs southeast along the Bay of Naples. To reach the ruins of Herculaneum, head a couple of kilometres past the town of Portico and follow the signs to car parks near the site. From Sorrento, head north along the SS145, and then east along the SS18.

VINTAGE VILLAS

The suburb of **Oplontis** (📱081 857 53 47; www.pompeiisites.org; Via dei Sepolcri, Torre Annunziata; adult/reduced incl Boscoreale €7/2; ⏰8.30am-7.30pm, last entry 6pm Apr-Oct, 8.30am-5pm, last entry 3.30pm Nov-Mar; 🚉Circumvesuviana to Torre Annunziata) was buried beneath the streets of Torre Annunziata, and only two of its houses have been unearthed. Villa Poppaea, the only one open to the public, has outstanding, richly coloured 1st-century wall paintings in the *triclinium* (dining room) and *caldarium* (hot bathroom) in the west wing. Marking the villa's eastern border is a garden with an envy-inducing swimming pool (17m by 61m). The villa is a straightforward 300m walk from Torre Annunziata Circumvesuviana train station.

South of Oplontis, **Stabiae** (📱081 857 53 47; www.pompeiisites.org; Via Passeggiata Archeologica, Castellammare di Stabia; ⏰8.30am-7.30pm, last entry 6pm Apr-Oct, 8.30am-5pm, last entry 3.30pm Nov-Mar; 🚉Circumvesuviana to Via Nocera) stood on the slopes of the Varano hill overlooking what was then the sea and is now modern Castellammare di Stabia. You can visit two villas: the 1st-century-BC Villa Arianna and the larger Villa San Marco. Neither is in mint condition, but the frescoes in Villa Arianna suggest that it must once have been quite something. Stabiae is a 1.1km walk south of Via Nocera Circumvesuviana station.

Some 3km north of Pompeii, the archaeological site of **Boscoreale** (📱081 857 53 47; www.pompeiisites.org; Via Settetermini; adult/reduced incl Oplontis €7/2; ⏰8.30am-7.30pm, last entry 6pm Apr-Oct, 8.30am-6.30pm, last entry 5pm Nov-Mar; 🚉Circumvesuviana to Villa Regina–Antiquarium) consists of a rustic country villa dating back to the 1st century BC, and a fascinating antiquarium showcasing artefacts from the surrounding region. Among the more unusual items on display are shreds of Roman fabric, eggshells from Pompeii and a carbonised loaf of bread. The ancient villa itself is currently inaccessible, though clearly visible from the grounds.

Mt Vesuvius

Rising formidably beside the Bay of Naples, Mt Vesuvius forms part of the Campanian volcanic arch, a string of active, dormant and extinct volcanoes that include the Campi Flegrei's Solfatara and Monte Nuovo, and Ischia's Monte Epomeo. Infamous for its explosive Plinian eruptions and surrounding urban sprawl, it's also one of the world's most carefully monitored volcanoes. Another full-scale eruption would be catastrophic. More than half a million people live in the so-called 'red zone', the area most vulnerable to pyroclastic flows and crushing pyroclastic deposits in a major eruption. Yet, despite government incentives to relocate, few residents are willing to leave.

 Sights

Mt Vesuvius
VOLCANO

(📱081 239 56 53; www.parconazionaledelvesuvio.it; crater adult/reduced €10/8; ⏰crater 9am-6pm Jul & Aug, to 5pm Apr-Jun & Sep, to 4pm Mar & Oct, to 3pm Nov-Feb, ticket office closes 1hr before crater) Vesuvius has blown its top more than 30 times. However, the views from the crater, which take in the Bay of Naples and part of the Apennine Mountains, are spectacular and compelling. Vesuvius is the focal point of the **Parco Nazionale del Vesuvio** (Vesuvius National Park), with nine nature walks around the volcano – download a simple map from the park's website. **Horse Riding Tour Naples** (📱345 8560306; www.horseridingnaples.com; guided tour €60) runs daily horse-riding tours.

The mountain is widely believed to have been higher than it currently stands, claiming a single summit rising to about 3000m rather than the 1281m of today. Its violent outburst in AD 79 not only drowned Pompeii in pumice and pushed the coastline back several kilometres but also destroyed much of the mountain top, creating a huge caldera and two new peaks. The most destructive explosion after that of AD 79 was in 1631, while the most recent was in 1944.

If travelling by car, exit the A3 at Ercolano Portico and follow signs for the Parco Nazionale del Vesuvio. From the summit car park (€5), a shuttle bus (return €3) reaches the ticket office and entry point further up the volcano.

Pompeii

Modern-day Pompeii (Pompei in Italian) may feel like a nondescript satellite of Naples, but it's here that you'll find Europe's most compelling archaeological site: the ruins of Pompeii. Sprawling and haunting, the site is a stark reminder of the destructive forces that lie deep inside Vesuvius.

◉ Sights

★ Ruins of Pompeii ARCHAEOLOGICAL SITE

(☑ 081 857 53 47; www.pompeiisites.org; entrances at Porta Marina & Piazza Anfiteatro; adult/reduced €15/2; ⊙ 9am-7.30pm Mon-Fri, from 8.30am Sat & Sun, last entry 6pm Apr-Oct, 9am-5.30pm Mon-Fri, from 8.30am Sat & Sun, last entry 3.30pm Nov-Mar; ☒ Circumvesuviana to Pompei Scavi–Villa dei Misteri) The ghostly ruins of ancient Pompeii make for one of the world's most engrossing archaeological experiences. Much of the site's value lies in the fact that the town wasn't simply blown away by Vesuvius in AD 79 but buried under a layer of *lapilli* (burning fragments of pumice stone). The result is a remarkably well-preserved slice of ancient life, where visitors can walk down Roman streets and snoop around millennia-old houses, temples, shops, cafes, amphitheatres and even a brothel.

The origins of Pompeii are uncertain, but it seems likely that it was founded in the 7th century BC by the Campanian Oscans. Over the next seven centuries, the city fell to the Greeks and the Samnites before becoming a Roman colony in 80 BC.

In AD 62, a mere 17 years before Vesuvius erupted, the city was struck by a major earthquake. Damage was widespread and much of the city's 20,000-strong population was evacuated. Fortunately, many had not returned by the time Vesuvius blew, but 2000 men, women and children perished nevertheless.

After its catastrophic demise, Pompeii receded from the public eye until 1594, when the architect Domenico Fontana stumbled across the ruins while digging a canal. Exploration proper, however, didn't begin until 1748. Audio guides are a sensible investment (€8) and a good guidebook will also help – try *Pompeii*, published by Electa Napoli.

Maintenance work is ongoing, with new discoveries unearthed regularly.

Porta Marina GATE

The ruin of Pompeii's main entrance is at Porta Marina, the most impressive of the seven gates that punctuated the ancient town walls. A busy passageway now, as it was then, it originally connected the town with the nearby harbour, hence the gateway's name.

Foro ARCHAEOLOGICAL SITE

A huge rectangle flanked by limestone columns, the *foro* (forum) was ancient Pompeii's main piazza, as well as the site of gladiatorial games before the Anfiteatro (p71) was constructed. The buildings surrounding the forum are testament to its role

DIEGO FIORE/SHUTTERSTOCK ©

Teatro Grande (p71), Pompeii

Tragedy in Pompeii

24 AUGUST AD 79

8am Buildings including the ❶ **Terme Suburbane** and the ❷ **Foro** are still undergoing repair after an earthquake in AD 63 caused significant damage to the city. Despite violent earth tremors overnight, residents have little idea of the catastrophe that lies ahead.

Midday Peckish locals pour into the ❸ **Thermopolium di Vetutius Placidus**. The lustful slip into the ❹ **Lupanare**, and gladiators practise for the evening's planned games at the ❺ **Anfiteatro**. A massive boom heralds the eruption. Shocked onlookers witness a dark cloud of volcanic matter shoot some 14km above the crater.

3pm–5pm Lapilli (burning pumice stone) rains down on Pompeii. Terrified locals begin to flee; others take shelter. Within two hours, the plume is 25km high and the sky has darkened. Roofs collapse under the weight of the debris, burying those inside.

25 AUGUST AD 79

Midnight Mudflows bury the town of Herculaneum. Lapilli and ash continue to rain down on Pompeii, bursting through buildings and suffocating those taking refuge within.

4am–8am Ash and gas avalanches hit Herculaneum. Subsequent surges smother Pompeii, killing all remaining residents, including those in the ❻ **Orto dei Fuggiaschi**. The volcanic 'blanket' will safeguard frescoed treasures like the ❼ **Casa del Menandro** and ❽ **Villa dei Misteri** for almost two millennia.

TOP TIPS

➡ Visit in the afternoon.
➡ Allow three hours.
➡ Wear comfortable shoes and a hat.
➡ Bring drinking water.
➡ Don't use flash photography.

Villa dei Misteri
Home to the world-famous *Dionysiac Frieze* fresco. Other highlights at this villa include *trompe l'oeil* wall decorations in the *cubiculum* (bedroom) and Egyptian-themed artwork in the *tablinum* (reception).

Villa di Diomede

Casa del Poeta Tragico

Porta Ercolano

Casa del Fauno

Basilica

Tempio di Apollo

Porta Marina

Terme del Foro

Macellum

Teatro Grande

Quadriportico dei Teatri

Porta di Stabia

Teatro Piccolo

Foro
An ancient Times Square of sorts, the forum sits at the intersection of Pompeii's main streets and was closed to traffic in the 1st century AD. The plinths on the southern edge featured statues of the imperial family.

Lupanare

The sex workers at this brothel were often slaves of Greek or Asian origin. Mattresses once covered the stone beds and the names engraved in the walls are possibly those of the workers and their clients.

Thermopolium di Vetutius Placidus

The counter at this ancient snack bar once held urns filled with hot food. The *lararium* (household shrine) on the back wall depicts Dionysus (the god of wine) and Mercury (the god of profit and commerce).

Casa dei Vettii

Porta del Vesuvio

EYEWITNESS ACCOUNT

Pliny the Younger (AD 61–c 112) gives a gripping, first-hand account of the catastrophe in his letters to Tacitus (AD 56–117).

Porta di Nola

Casa della Venere in Conchiglia

Porta di Sarno

③

⑦

Grande Palestra

⑤

Tempio di Iside

⑥

Orto dei Fuggiaschi

The Garden of the Fugitives showcases the plaster moulds of 13 locals seeking refuge during Vesuvius' eruption – the largest number of victims found in any one area. The huddled bodies make for a moving scene.

Casa del Menandro

This dwelling most likely belonged to the family of Poppaea Sabina, Nero's second wife. A room to the left of the atrium features Trojan War paintings and a polychrome mosaic of people rowing down the Nile.

Anfiteatro

Magistrates, local senators and the games' sponsors and organisers enjoyed front-row seating at this veteran amphitheatre, home to gladiatorial battles and the odd riot. The parapet circling the stadium featured paintings of combat, victory celebrations and hunting scenes.

Old Pompeii

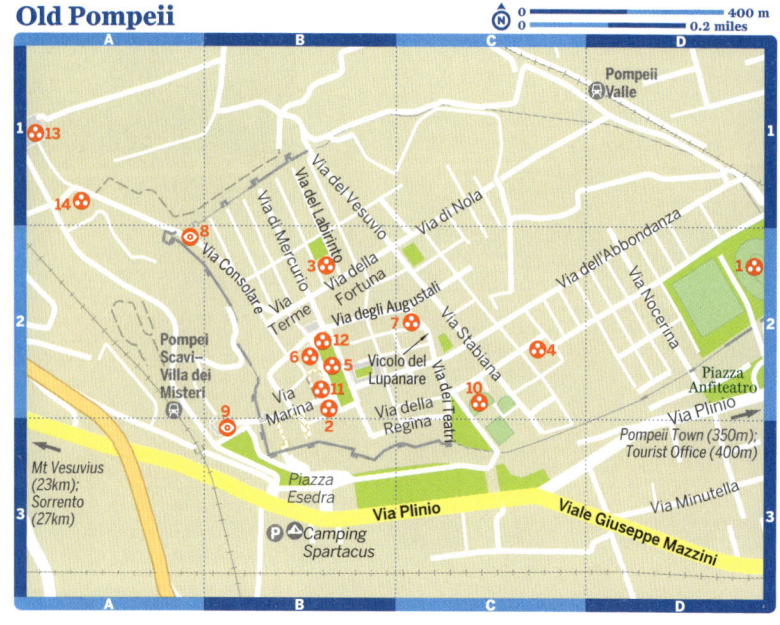

Old Pompeii

as the city's hub of civic, commercial, political and religious activity. At its northern end are the remains of the **Tempio di Giove** (Temple of Jupiter; Capitolium), the heart of religious life in Pompeii.

Basilica
ARCHAEOLOGICAL SITE

The basilica was the 2nd-century-BC seat of Pompeii's law courts and exchange. The semicircular apses would later influence the design of early Christian churches.

Tempio di Apollo
ARCHAEOLOGICAL SITE

The oldest and most important of Pompeii's religious buildings, the Tempio di Apollo (Temple of Apollo) largely dates from the 2nd century BC, including the striking columned portico. Fragments remain of an earlier version dating from the 6th century BC. The statues of Apollo and Diana (depicted as archers) on either side of the portico are copies; the originals are housed in Naples' Museo Archeologico Nazionale (p54).

Granai del Foro
ARCHAEOLOGICAL SITE

The Granai del Foro (Forum Granary) is now used to store hundreds of amphorae and a number of body casts that were made in the late 19th century by pouring plaster into the hollows left by disintegrated bodies. Among these casts is a pregnant slave; the belt around her waist would have displayed the name of her owner.

Lupanare
ARCHAEOLOGICAL SITE

The explicit frescoes at this ancient brothel provided visual 'inspiration' for clients. Once ready, visitors would indulge in one of the five rooms on the ground floor, each complete with a stone bed and latrine. Scan the walls for declarations of love and hope, written in various languages by the brothel's workers.

Teatro Grande
ARCHAEOLOGICAL SITE

The 2nd-century-BC Teatro Grande was a huge 5000-seat theatre carved into the lava mass on which Pompeii was originally built. The site hosts the annual **Pompeii Theatrum Mundi** (www.teatrostabilenapoli.it/pompeii-theatrum-mundi; ⊙ Jun-Jul), a summer season of classical theatre.

Casa del Menandro
ARCHAEOLOGICAL SITE

Better preserved than the larger Casa del Fauno, luxurious Casa del Menandro has an outstanding, elegant peristyle (a colonnade-framed courtyard) beyond its beautifully frescoed atrium. On the peristyle's far right side a doorway leads to a private bathhouse, lavished with exquisite frescoes and mosaics. The central room off the far end of the peristyle features a striking fresco of the ancient Greek dramatist Menander, after whom the rediscovered villa was named.

Anfiteatro
ARCHAEOLOGICAL SITE

Gladiatorial battles thrilled up to 20,000 spectators at the grassy *anfiteatro* (amphitheatre). Built in 70 BC, it's the oldest known Roman amphitheatre in existence. In 59 AD, the venue witnessed violent clashes between spectators from Pompeii and Nucera, documented in a fresco now found in Naples' Museo Archeologico Nazionale.

Casa del Fauno
ARCHAEOLOGICAL SITE

Pompeii's largest private house – covering an entire *insula* (city block) and claiming two atria at its front end (humbler homes had one), Casa del Fauno (House of the Faun) is named after the delicate bronze statue in the *impluvium* (shallow pool). It was here that early excavators found Pompeii's greatest mosaics, most of which are now in Naples' Museo Archeologico Nazionale. Valuable on-site originals include a beautiful, geometrically patterned marble floor.

Villa dei Misteri
ARCHAEOLOGICAL SITE

This restored, 90-room villa is one of the most complete structures left standing in Pompeii. The **Dionysiac frieze**, the most important fresco still on site, spans the walls of the large dining room. One of the biggest and most arresting paintings from the ancient world, it depicts the initiation of a bride-to-be into the cult of Dionysus, the

> **❶ TOURS**

You'll almost certainly be approached by a guide outside the ticket office. Authorised guides wear identification tags. If considering a guided tour of the ruins, reputable tour operators include **Yellowsudmarine Food & Art Tours** (☑ 329 1010328; www.yellowsudmarine.com; 2hr Pompeii guided tour €150, plus entrance fee) and **Walks of Italy** (www.walksofitaly.com; 3hr Pompeii guided tour per person €59).

Greek god of wine. A farm for much of its life, the villa's vino-making area is still visible at the northern end.

To get here follow Via Consolare northwest out of the town through **Porta Ercolano**. Continue past **Villa di Diomede** and you'll come to Villa dei Misteri.

🛏 Sleeping & Eating

Although the town of Pompeii has a number of mainly nondescript hotels, you're better off basing yourself in Sorrento or Naples and exploring the ruins as an easy day trip.

★President
CAMPANIAN €€€

(☑ 081 850 72 45; www.ristorantepresident.it; Piazza Schettini 12; meals €80, tasting menus €80-120; ⊙ noon-3.30pm & 7pm-late Tue-Sun; 🚆 FS to Pompei, Circumvesuviana to Pompei Scavi–Villa dei Misteri) At the helm of this Michelin-starred standout is charming owner-chef Paolo Gramaglia, whose passion for local produce, history and culinary whimsy translates into bread made to ancient Roman recipes, yellowtail carpaccio with bitter orange and citrus zest, lemon emulsion and buffalo mozzarella, or impeccably glazed duck breast lifted by vinegar cherries, orange sauce and nasturtium.

❶ Getting There & Away

If driving from Naples, head southeast on the A3, using the Pompei exit and following the signs to Pompei Scavi. Car parks are clearly marked and vigorously touted. Close to the ruins, **Camping Spartacus** (☑ 081 862 40 78; www.campingspartacus.it; Via Plinio 127) offers good-value, all-day parking (€5). This is a much cheaper option than the main car park located directly north of the Circumvesuviana train station.

From Sorrento, head north along the SS145, which connects to the A3 and Pompeii.

Sorrento & Around

Sorrento makes a good base for exploring the region's highlights: to the south is the best of the peninsula's unspoilt countryside, to the east is the Amalfi Coast, to the north lie Pompeii and other archaeological sites, and offshore is the fabled island of Capri.

SORRENTO

📞 081 / POP 16,400

A small resort with a big reputation, Sorrento is a town of lemons, high-pedigree hotels and plunging cliffs that cut through the heart of the historical core.

Tourism has a long history here. It was a compulsory stop on the 19th-century 'Grand Tour' and interest in the town was first sparked by the poet Byron, who inspired a long line of holidaying literary geniuses – including Goethe, Dickens and Tolstoy – to sample the Sorrentine air. The romance persists. Wander through Piazza Tasso on any given Sunday and you'll be exposed to one of Italy's finer *passeggiatas* (strolls), snaking past palatial hotels, magnificent marquetry shops and simple Campanian restaurants serving *gnocchi alla sorrentina* finished off with a shot of ice-cold *limoncello*.

🔴 Sights

Museo Correale di Terranova　　MUSEUM

(📞 081 878 18 46; www.museocorreale.it; Via Correale 50; adult/reduced €8/5; ⊙ 9.30am-6.30pm Mon-Sat, to 1.30pm Sun) East of the city centre, this wide-ranging museum is well worth a visit whether you're a clock collector, an archaeological egghead or into delicate ceramics. In addition to the rich assortment of 16th- to 19th-century Neapolitan arts and crafts (including extraordinary examples of marquetry), you'll discover Japanese, Chinese and European ceramics, clocks, fans, and ancient and medieval artefacts. Among these is a fragment of an ancient Egyptian carving uncovered in the vicinity of **Sedile Dominova** (Via San Cesareo).

Chiesa & Chiostro di San Francesco　　CHURCH

(📞 081 878 12 69; Via San Francesco; ⊙ 7am-7pm) Located next to the Villa Comunale Park, this church is best known for the peaceful

14th-century cloister abutting it, which is accessible via a small door from the church. The courtyard features an Arabic portico and interlaced arches supported by octagonal pillars. Replete with bougainvillea and birdsong, they're built on the ruins of a 7th-century monastery. Upstairs in the Sorrento International Photo School, the **Gallery Celentano** (☑344 0838503; www.raffaelecelentano.com; adult/reduced €3.50/free; ◷10am-9pm Mar-Dec) exhibits black-and-white photographs of Italian life and landscapes by contemporary local photographer Raffaele Celentano.

The cloisters host classical-music concerts in the summer.

Museo Bottega della Tarsia Lignea   MUSEUM
(☑081 877 19 42; Via San Nicola 28; adult/reduced €8/5; ◷10am-6.30pm Apr-Oct, to 5pm Nov-Mar) Since the 18th century, Sorrento has been famous for its *intarsio* (marquetry) furniture, made with elaborately designed inlaid wood. Some wonderful historical examples can be found in this museum, many of them etched in the once-fashionable picaresque style. The museum, housed in an 18th-century palace complete with beautiful frescoes, also has an interesting collection of paintings, prints and photographs depicting the town and the surrounding area in the 19th century.

Duomo   CATHEDRAL
(☑081 878 22 48; Corso Italia; ◷8am-12.30pm & 4.30-9pm) Sorrento's cathedral features a striking exterior fresco, a triple-tiered bell tower, four classical columns and an elegant majolica clock. Inside, take note of the marble bishop's throne (1573), as well as both the wooden choir stalls and stations of the cross, decorated in the local *intarsio* (marquetry) style. Although the cathedral's original structure dates from the 15th century, the building has been altered several times, most recently in the early 20th century when the current facade was added.

Marina Grande   HARBOUR
(Via Marina Grande) Noticeably detached from the main city and bereft of the hydrofoils and ferries that crowd Marina Piccola, this secluded former fishing village has a timeless maritime air not dissimilar to Marina Corricella on Procida. Bobbing fishing boats and pastel-coloured houses add character to a quarter that's known for its family-run

seafood restaurants. The marina also protects the closest thing in Sorrento to a *spiaggia* (beach).

Centro Storico   AREA
(Historic Centre; Corso Italia) A major hub for shops, restaurants and bars, recently pedestrianised Corso Italia is the main thoroughfare shooting east–west through the bustling *centro storico*. Duck into the side streets to the north and you'll find narrow lanes flanked by traditional green-shuttered buildings, interspersed with the occasional *palazzo* (mansion), piazza or church. Souvenir and antiques shops, fashion boutiques, trattorias and some fine old buildings also jostle for space in this grid of cobbled backstreets.

🏃 Activities

★ Nautica Sic Sic   BOATING
(☑081 807 22 83; www.nauticasicsic.com; Via Marina Piccola 43, Marina Piccola; ◷Apr-Oct) Seek out the best beaches by rented boat, with or without a skipper. This outfit rents a variety of motor boats, starting at around €50 per hour or from €150 per day plus fuel. It also organises boat excursions and wedding shoots.

Bagni Regina Giovanna   SWIMMING
Sorrento lacks a decent beach, so consider heading to Bagni Regina Giovanna, a rocky beach with clear, clean water about 2km west of town, amid the ruins of the Roman Villa Pollio Felix. It's possible to walk here (follow Via Capo), but wear good shoes as it's a bit of a scramble.

⭐ Festivals & Events

Sant'Antonino   RELIGIOUS
(◷14 Feb) The city's patron saint, Sant'Antonino, is remembered annually with processions and huge markets. The saint is credited with having saved Sorrento during WWII when Salerno and Naples were heavily bombed.

Settimana Santa   RELIGIOUS
(Holy Week) Famed throughout Italy; the first procession takes place at midnight on the Thursday preceding Good Friday, with robed and hooded penitents in white; the second occurs on Good Friday, when participants wear black robes and hoods to commemorate the death of Christ.

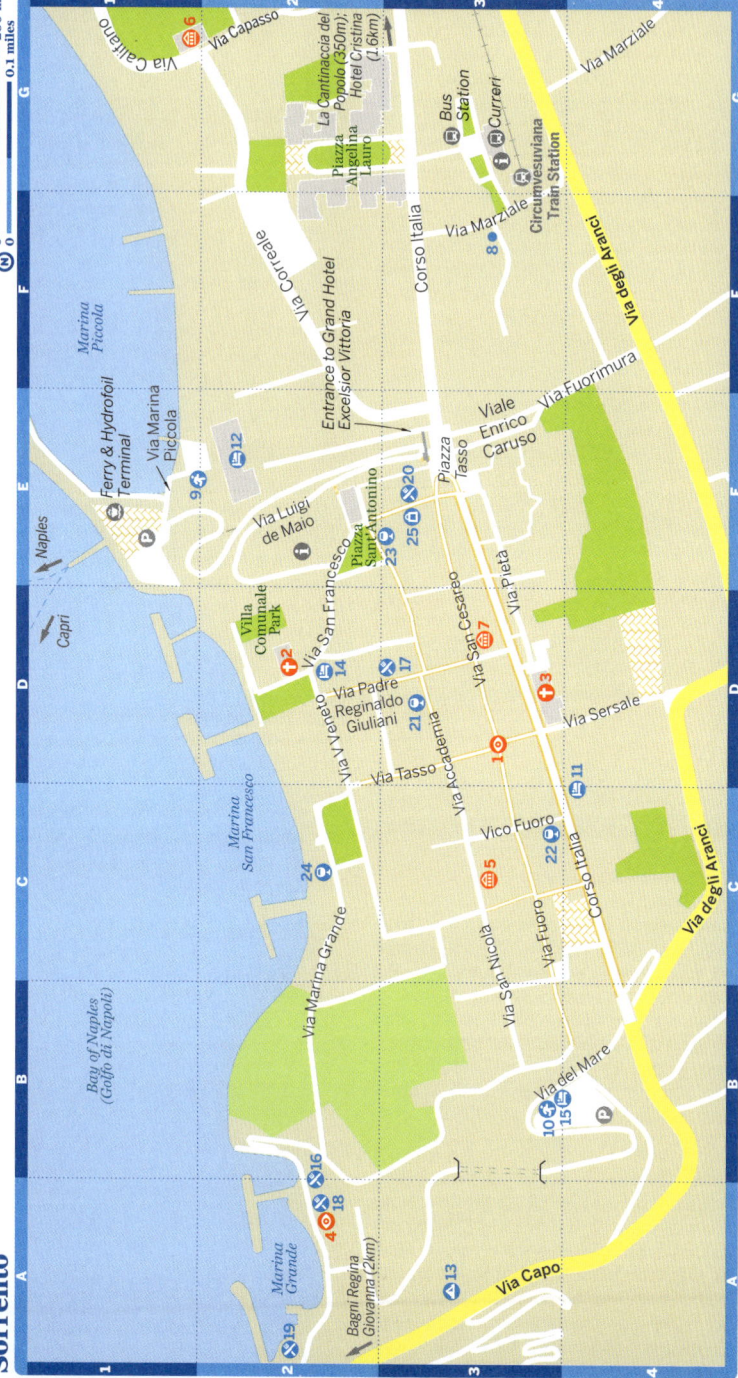

Sorrento

74

Sorrento

⊙ Sights
1 Centro Storico D3
2 Chiesa & Chiostro di San
  Francesco D2
3 Duomo D3
  Gallery Celentano .... (see 2)
4 Marina Grande A2
5 Museo Bottega della Tarsia
  Lignea C3
6 Museo Correale di Terranova G1
7 Sedile Dominova D3

⊕ Activities, Courses & Tours
8 Gelateria David F3
9 Nautica Sic Sic E1
10 Spa Ulysse Sorrento B3

🛌 Sleeping
11 Casa Astarita C4
12 Grand Hotel Excelsior Vittoria E2

13 Nube d'Argento A3
14 Palazzo Marziale D2
15 Ulisse B4

⊗ Eating
16 Da Emilia A2
17 L'Antica Trattoria D3
18 O'Puledrone A2
19 Soul & Fish A2
20 Zi'Ntonio E3

⊙ Drinking & Nightlife
21 Bollicine D3
22 Cafè Latino C3
23 D'Anton E3
24 La Pergola C2

⊙ Shopping
25 Stinga E3

🛌 Sleeping

Accommodation is thick on the ground in Sorrento, although if you're arriving in high summer (July and August), you'll need to book ahead. Most of the big city-centre hotels are geared towards package tourism and prices are correspondingly high. There are, however, some excellent choices, particularly on Via Capo, the coastal road west of the centre.

Ulisse   HOSTEL €
(☎ 081 877 47 53; www.ulissedeluxe.com; Via del Mare 22; dm from €35, d from €139; P ✴ 🛜 🛂) Although it calls itself a hostel, the Ulisse is about as far from a backpackers' pad as a hiking boot from a stiletto. Most rooms are plush, spacious affairs with swish if bland fabrics, gleaming floors and large en-suite bathrooms. There are two single-sex dorms, and quads for sharers. Breakfast is included in some rates but costs €10 with others.

There is an adjacent **wellness centre** (☎ 081 807 35 81; www.spaulysse.it; ☺ baths 11am-10pm Mon, Wed & Fri, 3-10pm Tue & Thu, 11am-8pm Sat, 10am-7pm Sun, massage centre 9am-8pm Mon-Sat, 10am-7pm Sun) where guests get to use the facilities for a daily rate of €10.

Nube d'Argento   CAMPGROUND €
(☎ 081 878 13 44; www.nubedargento.com; Via Capo 21; camping per 2 people, car & tent €26-42, 2-person bungalows €70-95, 4-person bungalows €100-130; ☺ late Mar-early Jan; 🛜 🛂) Remarkably central for a campground, this sloping affair set in a ravine above the Maria Grande has pitches and wooden chalet–style bungalows spread out beneath a canopy of olive trees – a source of much-needed summer shade – and the facilities are excellent. Kids in particular will enjoy the open-air swimming pool, table-tennis table, slides and swings.

Hotel Cristina   HOTEL €€
(☎ 081 878 35 62; www.hotelcristinasorrento.it; Via Privata Rubinacci 6, Sant'Agnello; d/tr/q from €150/220/240; ☺ Mar-Oct; P ✴ 🛜 🛂) Located high above Sant'Agnello, this hotel has superb views, particularly from the swimming pool. The spacious rooms have sea-view balconies and combine inlaid wooden furniture with contemporary flourishes such as Philippe Starck chairs. There's an in-house restaurant and a free shuttle bus to/from Sorrento's Circumvesuviana train station.

Casa Astarita   B&B €€
(☎ 081 877 49 06; www.casastarita.com; Corso Italia 67; d €90-140, tr €115-165; ✴ 🛜) Housed in an 18th-century *palazzo* on Sorrento's main strip, this charming B&B has a colourful, eclectic look with original vaulted ceilings, brightly painted doors and tiled floors. Its eight rooms are simple but well equipped, with breakfast served on a large rustic table in the B&B's central parlour.

★ Palazzo Marziale   BOUTIQUE HOTEL €€€
(☎ 081 807 44 06; www.palazzomarziale.com; Largo San Francesco 2; d/ste from €220/455; ✴ 🛜) From cascading vines, Chinese porcelain urns and Persian rugs in the lobby lounge, to antique furniture, *objets* and artworks in the hallways, and inlaid wood in the lift, this sophisticated, 11-room hideaway is big on details. The

family's elegant tastes extend to the rooms, resplendent with high ceilings, chaise longues and classy mattresses and linens.

★ Grand Hotel Excelsior Vittoria
HOTEL €€€

(☎ 081 877 71 11; www.exvitt.it; Piazza Tasso 34; d/ste from €500/650; P ❀ 🛜 🍽) A hotel for over 170 years, the grand old dame of Sorrento oozes belle-époque elegance. Huge potted palms adorn gilded public rooms awash with antique furniture. Rooms vary in size and style, ranging from tasteful simplicity to extravagant, frescoed opulence, but all have views of the hotel's gardens, dripping with crimson bougainvillea, or over the sea to Vesuvius.

Eating

The centre of town heaves with bars, cafes, trattorias, restaurants and even the odd kebab takeaway shop. Many places, particularly those with waistcoated waiters stationed outside (or eateries displaying sun-bleached photos of the dishes), are tourist traps serving bland food at inflated prices. Don't leave without a dose of *gnocchi alla sorrentina* (gnocchi with tomato sauce and mozzarella).

La Cantinaccia del Popolo
NEAPOLITAN €

(☎ 366 1015497; Vico Terzo Rota 3; meals €21; ⊗ 11am-3pm & 7-11pm Tue-Sun) Festooned with garlic and with cured hams hanging from the ceiling, this down-to-earth favourite proves that top-notch produce and simplicity are the keys to culinary success. A case in point is the *spaghetti al pomodoro,* a basic dish of pasta and tomato that bursts with flavour, vibrancy and balance. For extra authenticity, it's served directly to you in the pan.

La Cantinaccia also plies its own cured meats and some interesting Campanian cheeses straight out of the glass deli counter.

★ O'Puledrone
SEAFOOD €€

(☎ 081 012 41 34; www.opuledrone.com; Via Marina Grande 150; meals €30-35; ⊗ noon-3pm & 6.30pm-late Apr-Oct) The best fish you eat in Sorrento might be one you caught, a viable proposition at this congenial joint on the harbour at Marina Grande run by a cooperative of local fishermen. Let them take you out on a three-hour fishing trip (€70) and the chef will cook your catch and serve it to you with a carafe of wine.

★ Da Emilia
TRATTORIA €€

(☎ 081 807 27 20; www.daemilia.it; Via Marina Grande 62; meals €22-30; ⊗ noon-3pm & 6-10.30pm Mar-Nov; 👶) Founded in 1947 and still run by the same family, this is a friendly, fast-moving joint overlooking the fishing boats in Marina Grande. There's a large informal dining room, complete with youthful photos of former patron Sophia Loren, a romantic terrace by lapping waves, and a menu of straightforward dishes such as mussels with lemon, clam spaghetti and grilled calamari.

Soul & Fish
SEAFOOD €€

(☎ 081 878 21 70; Marina Grande; meals €38-46; ⊗ noon-2.30pm & 7-10.30pm, closed Nov-Easter; 🛜) Soul & Fish has a hipper vibe than Marina Grande's no-nonsense seafood restaurants. Your bread comes in a bag, your dessert might come in a Kilner jar and your freshly grilled fish with a waiter ready to slice it up before your eyes. The decor is more chic beach shack than sea-shanty dive bar, with wooden decks and director chairs.

Zi'Ntonio
ITALIAN €€€

(☎ 081 878 16 23; www.ristorantezintonio.it; Via Luigi De Maio 9-11; meals around €40; ⊗ noon-3.30pm & 6pm-midnight) Warm, buzzing and elegantly rustic, multilevel Zi'Ntonio draws everyone from local families and couples to

---

MAKE YOUR OWN GELATI

Impress your dinner-party pals with homemade Italian gelato by taking a course at **Gelateria David** (☎ 081 807 36 49; www.gelateriadavidsorrento.it; Via Marziale 19; ⊗ 8am-1am), a cream-of-the-crop gelateria run by the third generation in this ice-cream business. Classes (€12) last around an hour and culminate in your very own certificate. Times vary according to demand, so call or drop by to organise; they speak excellent English.

Specialities include fruity *profumo de Sorrento,* an orange, lemon and tangerine sorbet, and rum *babà.* Aside from mango, the gelateria uses only fresh fruit, which means that choices vary throughout the season. It also makes all the traditional, more commercial flavours, which are wonderfully creamy and bear little resemblance to most supermarket tubs.

Grand Hotel Excelsior Vittoria

clued-up out-of-towners. While earthy stand-outs include fried courgette flowers stuffed with buffalo mozzarella and basil, as well as a soul-coaxing lentil and escarole *zuppa* (soup), keep your belly empty if opting for the cult-status *risotto con crostacei,* a huge, flavour-packed paella-style seafood dish.

L'Antica Trattoria   ITALIAN €€€
(☑ 081 807 10 82; www.lanticatrattoria.com; Via Padre Reginaldo Giuliani 33; meals €60-80, fixed-price menus €49-90; ☉noon-11.30pm; ☑) Head to the upstairs terrace with its traditional tiles and trailing grape vines and you seem miles away from the alleyways outside. With a deserved reputation as the finest restaurant in town, this posh trattoria has a menu of many delicacies – courgette flowers, quail, and cod *au gratin* included – along with a resident mandolin player.

Drinking & Nightlife

★ D'Anton   LOUNGE
(☑ 333 1543706; Piazza Sant'Antonio 3/4; ☉10am-11pm mid-Mar–early Jan, to 1.30am summer; ☜) Welcome to a new and very Italian concept: a cocktail bar doubling up as an interior-design store. That elegant sofa you're sipping a negroni on is for sale. So is that glistening chandelier and that enchanting mirror. Add them to your drinks bill if you're feeling flush, or just admire the candelabras and lampshades over savoury antipasti and wicked chocolate-and-almond cake.

Bollicine   WINE BAR
(☑ 081 878 46 16; Via Accademia 9; ☉6pm-late Mar-Nov; ☜) The wine list at this unpretentious bar with a dark, woody interior includes all the big Italian names and a selection of interesting local labels. If you can't decide what to go for, the amiable bar staff will advise you. There's also a small menu of *panini* (sandwiches), bruschettas and one or two pasta dishes.

Cafè Latino   BAR
(☑ 081 877 37 18; www.cafelatinosorrento.it; Vico Fuoro 4a; ☉10am-1am Easter-Oct; ☜) Think locked-eyes-over-cocktails time. This is the place to impress your date with cocktails (€8) on the candlelit terrace, surrounded by orange, lemon and banana trees. Sip a spicy Hulk (vodka, grapefruit, sugar cane and jalapeño) or a glass of chilled white wine. If you can't drag yourselves away, you can also eat here (pizzas from €7, meals around €40).

La Pergola   BAR
(☑ 081 878 10 24; www.bellevue.it; Hotel Bellevue Syrene, Piazza della Vittoria 5; ☉10.30am-11pm) When love is in the air, put on your best Italian shoes and head for a predinner libation at the Hotel Bellevue Syrene's swoon-inducing terrace bar–restaurant. With its commanding clifftop view across the Bay of Naples towards Mt Vesuvius, it never fails to glam up an otherwise ordinary evening.

Shopping

Stinga
ARTS & CRAFTS

(☎ 081 878 11 65; www.stingatarsia.com; Via Luigi de Maio 16; ⊙9.30am-9.30pm) Well worth seeking out, this place sells distinctive inlaid-wood items made in Sorrento by the same family of craftspeople for three generations. The pieces are highly original, especially in their use of colour and design, which is often mosaic or geometric. Fine jewellery made by family member Amulè is also on display.

❶ Information

Main Tourist Office (☎ 081 807 40 33; www.sorrentotourism.com; Via Luigi de Maio 35; ⊙9am-7pm Mon-Sat, to 1pm Sun Jun-Oct, 9am-4pm Mon-Fri, to 1pm Sat Nov-May; 🖥) In the Circolo dei Forestieri (Foreigners' Club); lists ferry and train times. Ask for the useful publication *Surrentum*, published monthly from March to October.

❶ Getting There & Away

Coming from Naples and the north, take the A3 autostrada until Castellammare di Stabia; exit there and follow the SS145 south.

❶ Getting Around

TO/FROM THE AIRPORT

Naples International Airport (p64), also known as Capodichino, is the closest airport to Sorrento and the Amalfi Coast. A taxi from the airport to Sorrento costs around €85.

CAR & MOTORCYCLE

Autoservizi De Martino (☎ 081 878 28 01; www.admitaly.com/en; Via Parsano 8) Has cars from €54 a day, €280 per week, plus 50cc scooters from €23 for four hours.

Avis (☎ 081 878 24 59; www.avisautonoleggio.it; Corso Italia 322, Sant'Agnello; from €35 per day; ⊙8.30am-1.30pm & 3.30-7pm Mon-Fri, 9am-1pm Sat)

Hertz (☎ 081 807 16 46; www.hertz.it; Corso Italia 261b; from €33 per day; ⊙8.30am-1pm & 2-8pm Mon-Thu, 8.30am-1pm & 2-8pm Fri)

Parking

In midsummer, finding a parking spot can be a frustrating business, particularly as much of the parking on the side streets is for residents only and the city centre is closed to traffic for most of the day. There are well-signposted car parks near the ferry terminal, on the corner of Via degli Aranci and Via Renato, and heading west out of town near Via Capo (€2 per hour).

WEST OF SORRENTO

If you are here in midsummer, consider escaping the crowds by heading to the green hills around Sorrento. Known as the land of the sirens, in honour of the mythical maiden-monsters who were said to live on Li Galli (a tiny archipelago off the peninsula's southern coast), the area to the west of Sorrento is among the least developed and most beautiful in the country.

Tortuous roads wind their way through hills covered in olive trees and lemon groves, passing through sleepy villages and tiny fishing ports. There are magnificent views at every turn, the best from the high points overlooking Punta Campanella, the westernmost point of the Sorrento Peninsula. Offshore, Capri looks tantalisingly close.

HIKING THE PENINSULA

Forming a giant horseshoe between **Punta Campanella** and **Punta Penna**, the beautiful **Baia di Ieranto** (p81) is generally regarded as the top swimming spot on the Sorrento Peninsula. To get here you have two alternatives: take a boat, or walk from the village of Nerano, the steep descent forming part of a longer 6.5km hike from nearby Termini. This meandering path is just one of 20 (for a total of 110km) that cover the area linking tiny Sorrentine hamlets and weaving around the ample coastline. Distances range from tough all-day treks such as the 14.1km **Alta Via dei Monti Lattari** from the Fontanelle hills near Positano down to the Punta Campanella, to shorter walks suitable for all the family.

The trail network is complex and trail markings are sometimes unclear. Acquire a good map. The **Cart&guide** (www.carteguide.com) Amalfi Coast series, map #4 is a good bet. It costs €5 and is available from most bookshops and newsagents throughout the area.

Massa Lubrense

The first town you come to following the coast west from Sorrento is Massa Lubrense. Situated 120m above sea level, it's a disjointed place, comprising a small town centre and 17 *frazioni* (fractions or hamlets) joined by an intricate latticework of paths and mule tracks. For those without a donkey, there's a good network of regular SITA buses, but this is excellent walking country with the *due golfi* (the two gulfs of Naples and Salerno) rarely out of sight.

Sights & Activities

Chiesa di Santa Maria della Grazia
CHURCH

(Largo Vescovado; ⊘ 7am-noon & 4.30-8pm) The town's former cathedral, 16th-century Chiesa di Santa Maria della Grazia, is worth a quick look for its bright majolica-tiled floor, which would look *so* good in your kitchen back home. The church stands on the northern flank of the central Largo Vescovado. Don't forget your camera.

Marina della Lobra
HARBOUR

From central Largo Vescovado it's a 1.5km descent to this pretty little marina backed by ramshackle houses and verdant slopes. The marina is a good place to rent a boat, the best way of reaching the otherwise difficult-to-get-to bays and inlets along the coast.

Coop Marina della Lobra
BOATING

(☑ 081 808 93 80; www.marinalobra.com; Marina della Lobra; boat hire per hr from €40) A reliable boat-hire outfit, operating out of a kiosk by the car park. It also runs tours of Capri (€60).

Sleeping & Eating

Hotel Ristorante Primavera
HOTEL €

(☑ 081 878 91 25; www.laprimavera.biz; Via IV Novembre 3g; d €80-100; ⊘ Easter-Oct; ❄ 🤶) A welcoming family-run two-star, the Primavera has spacious, airy rooms with traditional Vietri tiles, light wood and white paint. Several have terraces with sunbeds, plus a table and chairs (rooms 101 to 103 are good choices). Bathtubs in most rooms are an unexpected treat. The bright terrace restaurant, with views stretching over orchards to the sea, serves typical local cuisine.

⭐ Casale Villarena
APARTMENT €€

(☑ 081 808 17 79; www.casalevillarena.it; Via Cantone 3, Nerano; 2-/4-person apt from €120/220; ⊘ Easter-Oct; 🅿 🎿) These family-friendly

Chiesa di Santa Maria della Grazia
CEZARY WOJTKOWSKI/SHUTTERSTOCK ©

apartments have good facilities, including a shared pool, a playground and a lovely beach within easy strolling distance. There are landscaped terraces with lemon trees, shady pergolas and such practical necessities as a laundry. The original property dates from the 18th century, but almost, the apartments are comfortable, spacious and simply, yet elegantly, furnished.

⭐ La Torre
SEAFOOD €€

(☑ 081 808 95 66; www.latorreonfire.it; Piazzetta Annunziata 7, Annunziata; meals €30-40; ⊘ 9am-midnight Mon & Wed-Thu, to 1am Fri-Sun Apr-Feb) 🌿 Not quite in Massa, but almost, La Torre has its berth in Annuziata, an attractive little *borgo* (medieval hamlet) on a hill overlooking the Gulf of Naples. Occupying a handsome old stone building next to a church, it specialises in 'slow' seafood such as amberjack grilled with Sorrento lemons or linguine with anchovies.

Funiculì Funiculà
SEAFOOD €€

(☑ 081 878 93 92; Via Fontanelle 16, Marina della Lobra; meals €32; ⊘ noon-3pm Tue-Sun, plus 7-11.30pm Sat & Sun Apr-Oct; 🚼) FF is a jack of all trades overlooking Marina della Lobra's dinky harbor where the parked cars are usually Fiat 500s and the moored boats are equally diminutive. Depending on your mood, choose between a cappuccino in the cafe or a plate of the local catch in the sit-down restaurant. If you're undecided, toss a coin – they're both good.

Ristorante Don Alfonso 1890

ℹ️ Information

Tourist Office (☎ 081 533 90 21; www.
massalubrenseturismo.it; Viale Filangieri 11;
⊘ 9.30am-1pm daily, plus 4.30-8pm Mon, Tue &
Thu-Sat) Can provide bus timetables and maps.

ℹ️ Getting There & Around

Massa Lubrense is an easy 20-minute drive from
Sorrento. Parking is a matter of trawling the
streets; there are some meters in the centre (€2
per hour).

Sant'Agata sui Due Golfi

Sant'Agata sui Due Golfi is the most famous of Massa Lubrense's 17 frazioni. It's
a tranquil place that manages to retain its
rustic charm despite a fairly heavy hotel
presence.

For hikers, this area offers around 22
marked and well-maintained trails, stretching a total length of some 110km (66 miles).
The tourist office can provide details. If you
fancy a relatively easy stroll that doesn't require a compass or hiking boots, there's a
picturesque 3km trail between Sorrento and
Sant'Agata. From Piazza Tasso in Sorrento,
venture south along Viale Caruso and Via
Fuorimura to pick up the Circumpiso foot-
path, marked in green on the walking maps
available from tourist offices. The walk
should take approximately one hour.

🔴 Sights

Convento del Deserto   MONASTERY, VIEWPOINT
(Monastero di San Paolo; ☎ 081 878 01 99; Via Deserto; ⊘ grounds 8am-7pm, viewpoint 10am-noon &
5-7pm summer, 10am-noon & 3-5pm winter) This
hulking convent is located 1.5km uphill from
the village centre. It was founded in the 17th
century by Carmelite friars, but since 1983
it has been home to a closed community of
Benedictine nuns. While the convent is of
only moderate interest, the 360-degree views
from the *belvedere* (rooftop terrace) really
make the knee-wearying hike worthwhile.

Chiesa di Sant'Agata   CHURCH
(Piazza Sant'Agata; ⊘ 8am-1pm & 5-7pm) Located
in the centre of the village, enjoy the cool
decorative interior of this 17th-century par-
ish church, famed for its polychrome marble
altar, an exquisite work of inlaid marble,
mother-of-pearl, lapis lazuli and malachite.

🛏️ Sleeping & Eating

Agriturismo Fattoria
Terranova   AGRITURISMO €
(☎ 081 533 02 34; www.fattoriaterranova.it; Via
Pontone 10; d/ste €85/100; ⊘ Mar-Dec; 🅿 ☻)
🍴 Stone floors, dried flowers hanging from
heavy wooden beams, and large wine barrels
artfully positioned – this great *agriturismo*
(farm stay) is the epitome of rural chic. The accommodation is in small apartments spread
over the extensively cultivated grounds. The

apartments are fairly simple, but the setting is delightful and the swimming pool is a welcome luxury.

Agriturismo Le Tore
AGRITURISMO €€

(☑ 081 808 06 37; www.agriturismosorrentoletore. com; Via Pontone 43; s €60-70, d €90-130, dinner €25-35; ⊙ Easter-early Nov; P @ 🙰) 🍴 Technically not a farm but a *masseria* (sprawling southern-Italian farming estates based on Roman villas), Le Tore guards 14 hectares of olive groves, producing widely lauded olive oil, sun-dried tomatoes and marmalade (among other products). Decidedly off the beaten track, its seven barn-like rooms have terracotta tiles, wooden furniture and plenty of rural appeal.

Lo Stuzzichino
NEAPOLITAN €

(☑ 081 533 00 10; www.ristorantelostuzzichino. it; Via Deserto 1a; pizzas from €5, meals €20, tasting menu €40; ⊙ Feb-Dec) 🍴 Stuzzichino means 'appetiser', but you get far more than just starters at this Slow Food movement–affiliated restaurant with gregarious host and owner Paolo de Gregorio at the helm. Loosen up with fish rolls stuffed with smoked cheese, or seafood stew with seasonal vegetables, and plunge in with the rare *gamberetti di Crapolla* (prawns).

★ Ristorante Don Alfonso 1890
MEDITERRANEAN €€€

(☑ 081 878 00 26; www.donalfonso.com; Corso Sant'Agata 11; meals €80, 6-course tasting menu €150; ⊙ 12.30-2.30pm & 7.30-11pm Wed-Sun Apr-late Oct; P) Don Alsonso is as much an experience as a meal – and a world-class one at that. Not only is the food exquisite, creative and true to its Sorrentino roots; it's also immaculately presented by genuinely friendly staff who treat every guest like they're visiting royalty.

🅘 Information

Tourist Office (☑ 081 533 01 35; Corso Sant'Agata 25; ⊙ 9am-1pm & 5.30-9pm) For information on the village and surrounding countryside, stop by this small office on the main square.

🅘 Getting There & Around

Follow the SS145 west from Sorrento for about 7km until you see signs off to the right. There is generally street parking available, although August can be busy, especially in the evening.

Marina del Cantone

Round the coast from Massa Lubrense, a beautiful hiking trail leads down from **Nerano** to the clear, placid **Baia di Ieranto** and Marina del Cantone. This unassuming village with a small pebble beach is not only a lovely, tranquil place to stay but also one of the area's prime dining spots: VIPs regularly sail over from Capri to eat here.

A popular diving destination, the protected waters here are part of an 11-sq-km reserve called the **Punta Campanella** (www. puntacampanella.org); it supports a healthy marine ecosystem, with flora and sea creatures flourishing in underwater grottoes.

Nettuno Diving
DIVING

(☑ 081 808 10 51; www.divingsorrento.com; Via Vespucci 39; 1/2 dives €65/110; ⊙ 8am-7pm; 🚻) One of the Sorrento Peninsula's best diving operators, based at the Nettuno campground (p82). Instructors are authorised to access the Punta Campanella protected marine park on designated days. There are 20 dive sites within 20 minutes of the centre and it can also organise night dives (€10 supplement), open-water courses (€395) and snorkelling trips to Capri (€35).

CELEB-STYLE SEAFOOD

The only one of the marina's restaurants directly accessible from the sea, **Lo Scoglio** (☑ 081 808 10 26; www.hotelloscoglio.com; Piazza delle Sirene 15, Marina del Cantone; meals €60; ⊙ 12.30-5pm & 7.30-11pm) attracts a steady ripple of visiting celebs. Johnny Depp, Stephen Spielberg and Sienna Miller are all recent diners, while Elton John, Rod Stewart and Michael Caine have posed for pics (on display) in the past.

The locale is certainly memorable – a glass pavilion on a wooden jetty built around a kitsch fountain spurting into a pond full of fish – and the food is top notch (and priced accordingly). Although you can eat *ravioli alla caprese* and steak here, you'd be sorry to miss the superb seafood. Sample such saltwater specialities as a €30 antipasto of raw seafood on ice, followed by the local classic: *spaghetti al riccio* (spaghetti with sea urchins). Despite the whiff of glamour surrounding the clientele, this is an unpretentious, family-run place, complete with grandma keeping a watchful eye on the till.

Villaggio Residence
Nettuno   CAMPGROUND, APARTMENT €

(✆081 808 10 51; www.villaggionettuno.it; Via A
Vespucci 39; camping 2 people, car & tent €41.50,
bungalows €110-130, apt from €150; ☯Mar-early
Nov; P❉@☎☀) 🅿 Marina's campground
– in the terraced olive groves by the entrance
to the village – offers an array of accommodation options, including campsites, mobile
homes and (best of all) apartments in a
16th-century tower for two to five people. It's
a friendly, environmentally sound place with
excellent facilities and a comprehensive list
of activities.

EAST OF SORRENTO

More developed and less appealing than the
coast west of Sorrento, the area to the east
of town protects the district's longest sandy
beach, Spiaggia di Alimuri, at Meta, and the
Roman villas at Castellammare di Stabia.
From Castellammare you can catch a cable
car to the top of Monte Faito (1092m).

Vico Equense

Vico Equense (Vico) is a small clifftop town
about 10km northeast of Sorrento and just
five stops away via the Circumvesuviana
train. This is a laid-back, authentic place
worth a quick stopover, if only to sample
some of the famous pizza by the metre.

Chiesa dell'Annunziata   CHURCH

(Via Vescovado; ☯10am-noon Sun) Vico's clifftop
former cathedral is the only Gothic church
on the Sorrento Peninsula. Little remains
of the original 14th-century structure other
than the lateral windows near the main altar
and a few arches in the aisles. In fact, most
of what you see today, including the chipped
pink-and-white facade, is 17th-century
baroque.

In the sacristy, check out the portraits of
Vico's bishops, all of whom are represented
here except for the last one, Michele Natale, who was executed for supporting the
ill-fated 1799 Parthenopean Republic. His
place is taken by an angel with its finger to
its lips, an admonishment to the bishop to
keep his liberal thoughts to himself.

Ristorante &
Pizzeria da Gigino   PIZZA €

(✆081 879 83 09; www.pizzametro.it; Via Nicotera
15; pizza per metre €28-38; ☯noon-1.30am; ☎🚻)
Run by the five sons of pizza king Gigino
Dell'Amura, who introduced pizza by the
metre to the world, this giant cafeteria-like
pizzeria – the self-proclaimed 'university
of pizza' – produces kilometres of top-notch
pizza each day in four huge ovens. A metre
of pizza is enough to feed five hungry diners,
with a large selection of toppings, both traditional and more creative.

Although the place seats around 400 people, you may still have to wait for a table. No
reservations are taken.

ⓘ Information

Tourist Office (✆331 310 20 09; www.
prolocovicoequense.it; Via San Ciro 2; ☯9am-
2pm & 3-8pm Mon-Sat, 9.30am-1.30pm Sun)
General information on the area's attractions is
available from this helpful office near the main
square.

HISTORIC HAMLETS

Dotted around Vico's surrounding hills are a number of ancient hamlets, known as
casali. Untouched by mass tourism, they offer a glimpse into a rural way of life that has
changed little over the centuries. You'll need your wheels to get to them. From Vico, take
Via Roma and follow Via Rafaelle Bosco, which passes through the *casali* before circling
back to town. Highlights include **Massaquano** and the Capella di Santa Lucia (open on
request), famous for its 14th-century frescoes from the school of Giotto di Bondone (recognised as the forerunner of modern Western painting). **Moiano** is also worth checking
out; an ancient path from here leads to the summit of Monte Faito. And then there is
Santa Maria del Castello, with its fabulous views towards the southeast.

Three kilometres to the west of Vico, **Marina di Equa** stands on the site of the
Roman settlement of Aequa. Among the bars and restaurants lining the popular
pebble beaches you can still see the remains of the 1st-century-AD Villa Pezzolo, as
well as a defensive tower, the Torre di Caporivo, and the Gothic ruins of a medieval
limestone quarry.

RUI VALE SOUSA/SHUTTERSTOCK ©

Seggiovia del Monte Solaro

CAPRI

081 / POP 14,120

Capri is beautiful – seriously beautiful. There's barely a grubby building or untended garden to blemish the splendour. Steep cliffs rise majestically from an impossibly blue sea; elegant villas drip with wisteria and bougainvillea; even the trees seem to be carefully manicured.

Long a preserve of celebrities and the super-rich, this small, precipitous island off the west end of the Sorrento Peninsula has a tangible deluxe feel. Your credit card can get a lot of exercise in its expensive restaurants and museum-quality jewellery shops – a cappuccino alone can cost €7. But, regardless of this, Capri is worth visiting, whatever your budget. Glide silently up craggy Monte Solaro on a chairlift. Relive erstwhile poetic glories in Villa Lysis. Find a quiet space in the sinuous lanes of Anacapri. In the process, you'll enjoy some sublime moments.

⦿ Sights

★ Seggiovia del Monte Solaro   CABLE CAR

(081 837 14 38; www.capriseggiovia.it; Via Caposcuro; single/return €8/11; 9.30am-5pm May-Oct, 9am-4pm Mar & Apr, to 3.30pm Nov-Feb) Sitting in an old-fashioned chairlift above the white houses, terraced gardens and hazy hillsides of Anacapri as you rise to the top of Capri's highest mountain, the silence broken only by a distant dog barking or your own sighs of contentment, has to be one of the island's most sublime experiences. The ride takes an all-too-short 13 minutes, but when you get there, the views, framed by dismembered classical statues, are outstanding.

★ Villa Jovis   RUINS

(Jupiter's Villa; Via A Maiuri; adult/reduced €6/4; 10am-7pm Jun-Sep, to 6pm Apr, May & Oct, to 4pm Mar, Nov & Dec, closed Jan & Feb) Villa Jovis was the largest and most sumptuous of 12 Roman villas commissioned by Roman Emperor Tiberius (AD14–37) on Capri, and his main island residence. This vast complex, now reduced to ruins, famously pandered to the emperor's supposedly debauched tastes, and included imperial quarters and extensive bathing areas set in dense gardens and woodland. It's located a 45-minute walk east of Capri Town along Via Tiberio.

Grotta Azzurra   CAVE

(Blue Grotto; €14; 9am-5pm) Capri's most famous attraction is the Grotta Azzurra, an unusual sea cave illuminated by an otherworldly blue light. The easiest way to visit is to take a **boat tour** (081 837 56 46; www.motoscafisticapri.com; Private Pier 0; Grotta Azzurra/island trip €15/€18) from Marina Grande; tickets include the return boat trip, but the rowing boat into the cave and admission are paid separately. Beautiful though it is, the Grotta is extremely popular in the summer. The crowds, coupled with long waiting times and tip-hungry guides, can make the experience underwhelming for some.

83

SOOTHING ISLAND HIKES

Away from the boutiques, yachts and bikinis, Capri offers some soul-lifting hikes. Favourite routes include from Arco Naturale to the Punta dell'Arcera (1.2km, 1¼ hours), best tackled in this direction to avoid a final climb up to Arco Naturale. Another popular route is from Anacapri to Monte Solaro (2km, two hours), the island's highest point. If you don't fancy an upward trek, take the *seggiovia* (chairlift) up and walk down.

Giardini di Augusto   GARDENS

(Gardens of Augustus; €1; ⊙ 9am-7.30pm summer, reduced hours rest of year) As their name suggests, these gardens near the Certosa di San Giacomo were founded by Emperor Augustus. Rising in a series of flowered terraces, they lead to a lookout point offering breathtaking views over to the **Isole Faraglioni**, a group of three limestone stacks rising out of the sea.

🛏 Sleeping & Eating

⭐ Casa Mariantonia   BOUTIQUE HOTEL €€

(☑ 081 837 29 23; www.casamariantonia.com; Via Orlandi 80, Anacapri; d €120-300; ⊙ late Mar-Oct; P ❋ ☎ ☒) A family-run boutique hotel with a history (*limoncello di Capri* was supposedly invented here), boasting nine fabulous rooms, a giant swimming pool, a prestigious restaurant and a heavyweight list of former guests – philosopher Jean-Paul Sartre among them. If the tranquillity, lemon groves and personal *pensione* feel doesn't sooth your existential angst, nothing will.

⭐ Capri Palace   HOTEL €€€

(☑ 081 978 01 11; www.capripalace.com; Via Capodimonte 2b, Anacapri; d/ste from €410/1070; ⊙ mid-Apr–mid-Oct; ❋ ☎ ☒) This really lives up to the 'palace' in its name – a regal mix of chicness, opulence and unashamed luxury that takes the concept of *la dolce vita* to dizzying heights. Lily-white communal areas set the scene for the lavish guestrooms – some even have their own terraced garden and private plunge pool with Warhol-esque motifs decorating the tiles.

⭐ La Minerva   BOUTIQUE HOTEL €€€

(☑ 081 837 70 67; www.laminervacapri.com; Via Occhio Marino 8, Capri Town; d €190-650; ⊙ late Mar-early Nov; ❋ ☎ ☒) This gleaming establishment is a model of Capri style and considered by many to be one of the best hotels in Italy. The 19 rooms, which cascade down the hillside, feature ravishing blue and white ceramic tiles, silk drapes and cool 100% linen sheets, while terraces come with sun loungers, jacuzzis and obligatory sea views.

⭐ La Palette   ITALIAN €€

(☑ 081 837 72 83; www.lapalette.it; Via Matermània 36; meals from €35; ⊙ 11am-midnight Apr-early Nov) Local Caprese ingredients are combined into the most flavour-filled, creative dishes possible here. Expect the delights of zucchini flowers stuffed with ricotta, fresh and tangy octopus salad, and an aubergine *parmigiana* that seems to taste so much better than everyone else's. An easy 10-minute walk from Capri Town, it has swooningly romantic bay views.

⭐ Il Geranio   SEAFOOD €€€

(☑ 081 837 06 16; www.geraniocapri.com; Via Matteotti 8, Capri Town; meals €45-50; ⊙ noon-3pm & 7-11pm mid-Apr–mid-Oct) Time to pop the question or quell those predeparture blues? The terrace at this sophisticated spot offers heart-stealing views over the pine trees to Isole Faraglioni. Seafood is the speciality, particularly the salt-baked fish. Other fine choices include octopus salad and linguine with saffron and mussels. Book at least three days ahead for a terrace table in high season.

❶ Information

Post Office (www.poste.it; Via Roma 50, Capri Town; ⊙ 8.20am-7pm Mon-Fri, to 12.30pm Sat; ☎) Located just west of the bus terminal.

Tourist Office (☑ 081 837 06 34; www.capritourism.com; Banchina del Porto; ⊙ 8.30am-4.15pm, closed Sat & Sun Jan-Mar & Nov) Can provide a map of the island, plus accommodation listings, ferry timetables and other useful information.

❶ Getting There & Around

The two major ferry routes to Capri are from Naples and Sorrento, although there are also seasonal connections with Ischia and the Amalfi Coast (Amalfi, Positano and Salerno).

There are year-round boats to Capri from Naples and Sorrento. Timetables and fare details are available online at www.capritourism.com. From Sorrento jetfoils cost €17 to €18.50 and slower ferries €14.50.

On the island, buses run from Capri Town to/from Marina Grande, Anacapri and Marina Piccola. Single tickets cost €1.80 on all routes, including the funicular.

Amalfi Coast

Deemed by Unesco to be an outstanding example of a Mediterranean landscape, the Amalfi Coast is a beguiling combination of great beauty and gripping drama.

Positano

🖋 089 / POP 3915

Dramatic, deluxe and more than a little dashing, Positano is the Amalfi Coast's front-cover splash, with vertiginous houses tumbling down to the sea in a cascade of sun-bleached peach, pink and terracotta. No less photo-worthy are its steep streets and steps, flanked by wisteria-draped hotels, smart restaurants and fashionable retailers.

Look beyond the facades and the fashion, however, and you will find reassuring signs of everyday reality: crumbling stucco, streaked paintwork and even, on occasion, a faint whiff of drains. There's still a southern-Italian-holiday feel about the place, with sunbathers eating pizza on the beach, kids pestering parents for gelato, and chic *signore* from Milan browsing the boutiques. The fashionista history runs deep – *moda Positano* was born here in the '60s and the town was the first in Italy to import bikinis from France.

◉ Sights & Activities

Positano's most memorable sight is its pyramidal townscape, with pastel-coloured houses stacked up on the hillsides.

Getting around town is largely a matter of walking. If your knees can take the slopes, dozens of narrow alleys and stairways make strolling around relatively straightforward and joyously traffic-free. The easy option is to take the local bus to the top of the town and wind your way down on foot.

Chiesa di Santa Maria Assunta
CHURCH

(🖋 089 87 54 80; Piazza Flavio Gioia; ⊘ 9am-noon & 4-7pm Mon-Sat) Omnipresent in most Positano photos is the colourful majolica-tiled dome of its main church (and the town's only real sight). If you are visiting at a weekend you will probably have the added perk of seeing a wedding; it's one of the most popular churches in southern Italy for exchanging vows.

PLAN YOUR ROUTE
....

1 **Amalfi Coast** (p17) Passing through Positano then along the coast to Vietri sul Mare, this trip encapsulates fabulously picturesque towns with dizzying hairpin turns.

Positano

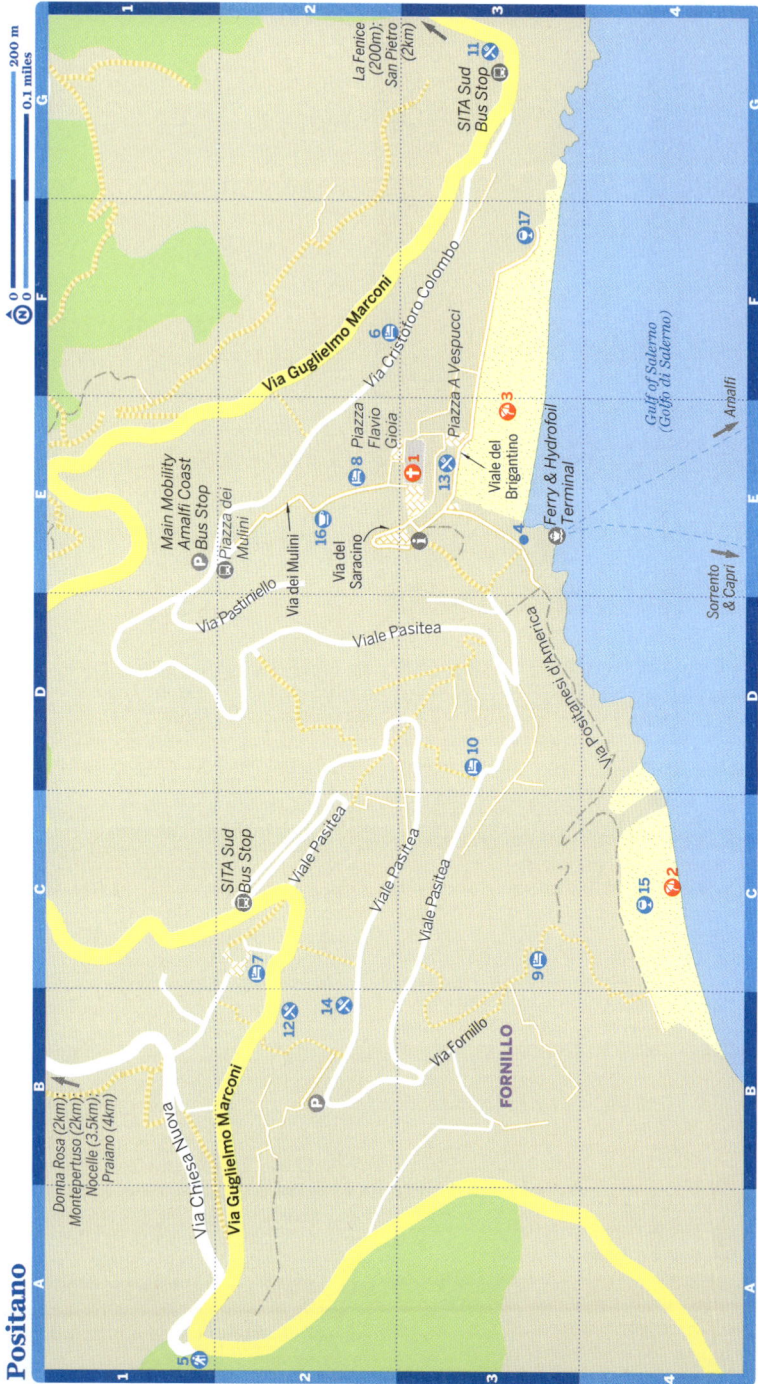

La Fenice (200m);
San Pietro (2km)

11 ⊗
SITA Sud
Bus Stop

17 🍴

Via Guglielmo Marconi

6 🍴

Via Cristoforo Colombo

Piazza A Vespucci

Piazza
Flavio
Gioia

8 🛏

1 🍴

13 ⊗

3 🛒

Viale del
Brigantino

Ferry & Hydrofoil
Terminal

4 ●

Via Positanesi d'America

ℹ

Main Mobility
Amalfi Coast
Bus Stop

🅿

Piazza dei
Mulini

16 🛏

Via del
Mulini

Via del
Saracino

Via Pastiniello

Viale Pasitea

Gulf of Salerno
(Golfo di Salerno)

Amalfi →

Sorrento
& Capri →

10 🛏

SITA Sud
Bus Stop

Viale Pasitea

Viale Pasitea

Viale Pasitea

15 🛏

2 🛒

7 🛏

9 🛏

12 ⊗

14 ⊗

🅿

Via Fornillo

FORNILLO

Donna Rosa (2km);
Montepertuso (2km);
Nocelle (3.5km);
Praiano (4km)

Via Chiesa Nuova

Via Guglielmo Marconi

5 ⊗

200 m
0.1 miles
0
0

Positano

The church is known for a 13th-century Byzantine *Black Madonna and Child* above the main altar. The icon was supposedly stolen from Constantinople by pirates and smuggled west.

A handsome 18th-century bell tower stands separate from the main church building in the piazza out front. During restoration works on the square and the crypt, a Roman villa was discovered.

Spiaggia Grande   BEACH
This beach might not be everyone's idea of a dream spot, with greyish sand covered by legions of bright umbrellas lined up like parked cars – and expensive cars at that. Hiring a chair and umbrella in the fenced-off areas costs around €20 per person per day (plus extra for showers). Fortunately, the crowded public areas are free and the toilets are spotlessly clean – as is the seawater.

Palazzo Murat   PALACE
(☑089 875 51 77; www.palazzomurat.it; Via dei Mulini 23) Just west of the Chiesa di Santa Maria Assunta, this *palazzo* (mansion) is now a luxury hotel. It may be beyond your budget to stay here, but you can still visit the balmy flower-filled courtyard, have a drink on the vine-draped patio and contemplate the short, tragic life of flamboyant Joachim Murat, the 18th-century French king of Naples who had the palace built as a summer residence for himself and his wife, Caroline Bonaparte.

Santa Maria del Castello Circuit   HIKING
For those travelling on foot, there's no real way out of Positano that doesn't involve climbing steep stone staircases – lots of 'em!

The advantage of this particular circuitous route is that it enjoys a bit of shade in its early stages as you plod heavenward amid a thick and gnarly holm-oak forest.

The walk starts on the main coast road (SS163) close to the Montepertuso turn-off by a ruined building and climbs steeply through trees before breaking into dryer Mediterranean scrub higher up. The coastal views open out as the path (#333a) traverses the hills above Positano, with the hulk of Monte Sant'Angelo standing sentinel in the background.

Turn left 2km up the ascent and then right at the top to join a wider trail towards the hike's high point; the tiny village of **Santa Maria del Castello** (670m) is accessible by diverting along a narrow, paved road. At this ancient crossing point around 5km into the hike, you'll find a small bar and a church. Take the narrow road back down to the main path; turn left (trail 333), proceed around the headland and then head right on a path that leads steeply down via a series of well-constructed staircases to Positano, visible in all its glory directly below. The walk ends beside the **Bar Internazionale** (Via Guglielmo Marconi 306; ⊙7am-1am) in Upper Positano. The total distance is 9km.

L'Uomo e il Mare   BOATING
(☑089 81 16 13; www.escursioniluomoeilmare.it; ⊙9am-8pm Easter-Oct) Offers a range of tours, including Capri and Amalfi day trips (from €65 to €80), out of a kiosk near the ferry terminal. It also organises private sunset tours to Li Galli, complete with champagne (from €200 for up to 12 people). Private tours should be organised at least a day in advance.

🛏 Sleeping

Villa Nettuno
HOTEL €

(☏089 87 54 01; www.villanettunopositano.it; Viale Pasitea 208; d €80-150; ☉Apr-Oct; ❄🛜) Hidden behind a barrage of perfumed foliage, lofty Villa Nettuno is not short on charm. Go for one of the original rooms in the 300-year-old part of the building, decked out in robust rustic decor and graced with a communal terrace. Bathrooms are a little old fashioned, but this place is all about the view.

Pensione Maria Luisa
PENSION €€

(☏089 87 50 23; www.pensionemarialuisa.com; Via Fornillo 42; d €129-179; ☉Mar-Oct; ❄@🛜) Carlo the ceramicist is the main man at Maria Luisa; he's an extremely congenial (and multilingual) host who'll make your stay in glitzy Positano feel pleasantly homely. Simple rooms have extravagant views over town (get one with a balcony) and handy fridges, and there's a small rooftop terrace.

It's in the Fornillo neighbourhood, a short walk via steps from the beach. Breakfast is €8 extra.

Hostel Brikette
HOSTEL €€

(☏089 87 58 57; www.hostel-positano.com; Via Guglielmo Marconi 358; dm €40-73, d €160-220; ☉mid-Mar–mid-Oct; ❄🛜) Though more expensive than most hostels, cheerful Brikette is relatively cheap by Positano standards as long as you opt for a dorm. The top-of-the-town building has wonderful views and a range of sleeping options, from doubles to three different types of dorm. Premium dorms have private bathrooms and terraces; all have handy bunk-side USB sockets and reading lights.

La Fenice
B&B €€

(☏089 87 55 13; www.lafenicepositano.com; Via Guglielmo Marconi 8; d €180; ☉Easter-Oct; ❄🛜⚓) With hand-painted Vietri tiles, high ceilings and the odd piece of antique furniture, the rooms at this friendly family-run place are simple but smart; most have their own balcony or terrace with dreamy views. As with everywhere in Positano, you'll need to be good at stomping up and down steps to stay here – it's 1km east of the town centre.

Albergo California
HOTEL €€

(☏089 87 53 82; www.hotelcaliforniapositano.it; Via Cristoforo Colombo 141; d €150-190; ☉Mar–mid-Oct; Ⓟ❄🛜) If you were to choose the best place to take a quintessential Positano photo, it might be from the balcony of this hotel. But the view isn't all you get. The rooms in the older part of this grand 18th-century palace are magnificent, with original ceiling friezes and decorative doors. New rooms are simply decorated but tasteful, spacious and minimalist.

★Hotel Palazzo Murat
HOTEL €€€

(☏089 87 51 77; www.palazzomurat.it; Via dei Mulini 23; d from €310; ☉late Mar-early Nov; ❄@🛜⚓) Positano personified. Hidden behind an ancient wall away from the tourists who surge along the pedestrian thoroughfares daily, this magnificent hotel occupies the 18th-century *palazzo* that the one-time king of Naples used as his summer residence. Rooms are regal quarters (one even has a crown over the bed) with sumptuous antiques, original oil paintings and gleaming marble.

🍴 Eating

Positano excels in deluxe restaurants with fine food and romantic settings, but you can also get by on a budget if you know where to look. Generally, the nearer you get to the seafront, the more expensive everything becomes. Many places close over winter, making a brief reappearance for Christmas and New Year.

★C'era Una Volta
TRATTORIA, PIZZA €

(☏089 81 19 30; Via Marconi 127; meals €20-30; ☉noon-3pm Wed-Mon, 6-11pm daily) Calling like a siren to any cash-poor budget traveller who thought Positano was for celebs only, this heroically authentic trattoria at the top of town specialises in honest, down-to-earth Italian grub. No need to look further than the *gnocchi alla sorrentina* (gnocchi in a tomato and basil sauce) and Caprese salad. Pizzas start at €4.50; beer €2. In Positano, no less!

It also runs a free shuttle to/from anywhere in Positano in the summer.

La Cambusa SEAFOOD €€

(☏ 089 87 54 32; www.lacambusapositano.com; Piazza Vespucci 4; meals €40; ☺ noon-11pm, closed Nov–mid-Dec; ☏) Sporting summery pastel hues and a seafront terrace, La Cambusa is on the front line, which, given the number of cash-rich tourists in these parts, could equal high prices for less-than-average food. Happily, that is not the case. Ingredients are top-notch and shine brightly in dishes such as homemade crab-filled ravioli and seafood risotto.

★ Casa Mele ITALIAN €€€

(☏ 089 81 13 64; www.casamele.com; Via Guglielmo Marconi 76; tasting menus €75-100; ☺ 7pm-midnight Tue-Sun Apr-Nov; ☏) Something of a rarity in this land of traditional trattorias, Casa Mele is one of those cool contemporary restaurants with a lengthy tasting menu and food presented as art – and theatre. The slick open kitchen is a window into a high-powered food laboratory from which emerge whimsical pastas, delicate fish in subtle sauces, and outstanding desserts. Service is equally sublime.

The restaurant's manifesto is inscribed on one wall in English: 'to eat is a necessity, but to eat intelligently is an art'. These people love food, and it shows.

Casa Mele also runs three-hour cooking courses (€120), which include a meal and wine; see the website for more details.

★ Donna Rosa ITALIAN €€€

(☏ 089 81 18 06; www.drpositano.com; Via Montepertuso 97-99, Montepertuso; meals €45-65; ☺ 11am-2pm & 5.30-10pm Wed-Mon Apr-Oct, closed lunch Aug) Once a humble trattoria, Donna Rosa is now considered an Amalfi Coast classic despite its out-of-the-way location in the village of Montepertuso. The reason? Jolly good food served by three generations of the original Rosa's family and a nod of admiration from that well-known food-campaigning Italophile, Jamie Oliver. Reservations are highly recommended for dinner and obligatory for lunch.

Next2 ITALIAN €€€

(☏ 089 812 35 16; www.next2.it; Viale Pasitea 242; meals €65, 6-course menu €80; ☺ 6.30-11pm Apr-Oct; ☏) Local produce and polished takes on tradition underscore sophisticated Next2. Standouts include the signature *conchiglioni ripieni di ragù alla bolognese e stracciatella*, shell-shaped pasta served with pork-mince *ragù* and *stracciatella* cheese. The kitchen boasts a top-range charcoal oven, put to fine use in dishes like tender octopus and mackerel with chickpea purée and cherry tomatoes. In summer, reserve a table on the terrace.

Positano (p85)

🍷 Drinking & Nightlife

La Zagara
CAFE

(📞 089 87 59 64; www.lazagara.com; Via dei Mulini 8; ⏰ 8am-10pm Apr–mid-Nov) Dating back to 1950, this is the quintessential Italian terrace, draped with foliage and flowers. Flanking the terrace is La Zagara's superb *pasticceria* (pastry shop; cakes from €3), serving both sweet and savoury bites, and especially famed for its *tiramisù al limone*.

Order something indulgent, kick back and indulge in a little Positano people-watching. DJs spin tunes on Friday and Saturday nights.

Music on the Rocks
CLUB

(📞 089 87 58 74; www.musicontherocks.it; Via Grotte dell'Incanto 51; ⏰ 10pm-4am Apr-Oct; 📶) This is one of the town's few genuine nightspots and one of the best clubs on the coast. The venue is dramatically carved into the tower at the eastern end of Spiaggia Grande. Join a lively crowd and some of the region's top DJs spinning anything from mainstream house to retro disco. Cover charge €10 to €30.

Da Ferdinando
BAR

(📞 089 87 53 65; Spiaggia dei Fornillo; ⏰ 10am-3am May-Oct) Caribbean-style bamboo beach bar that springs up every summer on Positano's smaller Fornillo beach. It rents out sunloungers and serves drinks and light snacks. Rock 'n' roll music creates a party mood after sunset.

ℹ️ Information

Tourist Office (📞 089 87 50 67; www.azienda turismopositano.it; Via Regina Giovanna 13; ⏰ 8.30am-5pm Mon-Sat, to 3pm Sun) Provides lots of information, from sightseeing and tours to transport information. Also supplies a free hiking map.

ℹ️ Getting There & Away

BOAT

Positano has excellent ferry connections to the coastal towns and islands between April and October from its ferry and hydrofoil terminal.

CAR & MOTORCYCLE

Positano is on the SS163 which connects with the A3 autostrada at Vietri sul Mare and the SS145 towards Sant'Agata sui Due Golfi. To hire a scooter, try **Positano Rent a Scooter** (📞 089 812 20 77; www.positanorentascooter.it; Viale Pasitea 99; per day from €60). Don't forget that you will need to produce a driving licence and passport.

Parking

Parking here is no fun in summer. There are some blue-zone parking areas (€3 per hour) and a handful of expensive private car parks. **Parcheggio da Anna** (Viale Pasitea 173; per hour €5) is located just before the Pensione Maria Luisa, at the top of town. Closer to the beach and town centre, **Di Gennaro** (Via Pasitea 1; per day €25) is near the bottom of Via Cristoforo Colombo.

CZUPPA/SHUTTERSTOCK ©

Praiano

A WALK TO FORNILLO

This gentle walk, with (hooray!) an acceptable number of steps, leads from Positano's main Spiaggia Grande to Spiaggia di Fornillo. Toss off the stilettos and don the trainers: Fornillo is more laid-back than its swanky spiaggia (beach) neighbour and is also home to a handful of summer beach bars, which can get quite spirited after sunset.

To reach here, head for the western end of Spiaggia Grande, by the ferry harbour, and climb the steps. Walk past the Torre Trasita, one of the coast's many medieval watchtowers built to warn inhabitants of pirate raids and now a private residence. Continue on as the path passes dramatic rock formations, tiny inlets of turquoise water and bobbing boats until you reach the appealing Fornillo beach in time to enjoy a long, cold drink or multiscoop ice cream.

Praiano

📶 089 / POP 2020

Praiano is glued to a steep bluff 120m above sea level and exploring it inevitably involves lots of steps. There are also several trails that start from town, including a dreamy walk – particularly romantic at sunset – that leaves from beside the San Gennaro church, descending due west to the **Spiaggia della Gavitelli**, via 300 steps, and carrying on to the medieval defensive Torre di Grado. The town also acts as an alternative starting point for the **Sentiero degli Dei** (Walk of the Gods; p94).

The spread-out settlement stretches east and down to the sea at **Marina di Praia**, a sheltered cove with restaurants, a beach and a couple of diving operators.

🛏 Sleeping & Eating

Fish and seafood dominate the menus in this old fishing town. Its most famous traditional dish is *totani e patate alla praianese*, a soulful combination of soft calamari rings, sliced potato, *datterini* tomatoes, garlic, croutons, *peperoncino* (chilli) and parsley.

Hotel Villa Bellavista   HOTEL €€

(📶 089 87 40 54; www.villabellavista.it; Via Grado 47; r €110-160; ☺ Apr-Oct; ❈ 🛜 🛋) Amid lush gardens that include a vast vegetable plot, this Praiano hotel has an old-fashioned charm with slightly stuffy furniture in the public areas and large, cool, but fairly bare rooms. Its appeal lies in the fabulous views from the spacious, flower-festooned terrace; the delightful pool, surrounded by greenery; and the tranquil setting.

Located on a narrow lane that leads to the Spiaggia della Gavitelli, the (signposted)

hotel is accessed via Via Rezzolo, which runs parallel to the SS163 coast road.

Hotel Onda Verde   HOTEL €€€

(📶 089 87 41 43; www.hotelondaverde.com; Via Terramare 3; d from €250; ☺ Apr-Oct; ℗ ❈ 🛜 🛋) The 'Green Wave' enjoys a commanding cliffside position overlooking secluded Marina di Praia. The interior is tunnelled into the stone cliff face, which makes it wonderfully cool in the height of summer. Elegant rooms have lashings of white linen, satin bedheads, Florentine-inspired furniture and majolica-tiled floors. Some spoil guests with terraces and deckchairs for panoramic contemplation. The restaurant comes highly recommended.

Da Armandino   SEAFOOD €€

(📶 089 87 40 87; Via Praia 1, Marina di Praia; meals €35; ☺ 1-4pm & 7pm-midnight Apr-Nov) Seafood-lovers should head for this widely acclaimed, no-frills restaurant located in a former boatyard on the beach at Marina di Praia. Da Armandino is great for fish fresh off the boat. There's no menu; just opt for the dish of the day – it's all excellent.

The holiday atmosphere and appealing setting – at the foot of sheer cliffs towering up to the main road – round things off nicely.

Onda Verde   ITALIAN €€

(📶 089 87 41 43; www.ondaverde.it; Via Terramare 3; meals €38; ☺ 12.30-9.30pm Apr-Nov) Part of the hotel with the same name, this restaurant is located halfway down the steep steps leading to the marina (just beyond the defensive tower). Sit outside for the best views of the bay. The food here reflects an innovative take on traditional cuisine and includes a plentiful choice of salads – just the thing on a sizzling summer's day.

🍷 Drinking & Nightlife

★ Africana Famous Club
CLUB

(☑089 81 11 71; www.africanafamousclub.com; Via Terramare 2; ◷10pm-late May-Sep, bar opens 8pm; ☎) All Amalfi nightlife converges in the unlikely setting of Marina di Praia. But this is no run-of-the-mill nightclub: Africana's been going since the '60s, when Jackie Kennedy was a regular guest. It has an extraordinary cave setting (complete with natural blowholes), a mix of DJs and live music, plus a glass dance floor with fish swimming beneath your feet. Cover charge €10 to €35.

ℹ️ Information

Tourist Office (☑089 87 45 57; www.praiano. org; Via G Capriglione 116b; ◷9am-1pm & 4.30-8.30pm Mon-Sat) Can provide maps and information for the area's hiking trails.

ℹ️ Getting There & Away

SITA Sud (☑342 6256442; www.sita sudtrasporti.it; Piazza Flavio Gioia) runs up to 27 daily buses to Sorrento (€2.40, 1¼ hours). It also runs up to 25 daily services to Amalfi (€1.30, 25 minutes) from where buses continue east to Salerno. Reduced services on Sunday.

Marina di Furore

Marina di Furore, a tiny fishing village, was once a busy little commercial centre, although it's difficult to believe that today. In medieval times, its unique natural position freed it from the threat of foreign raids and provided a ready source of water for its flour and paper mills.

Originally founded by Romans fleeing barbarian incursions, it sits at the bottom of what's known as the Fiordo di Furore, a giant cleft that cuts through the Lattari mountains. The mouth of the fjord is crossed by an arched stone bridge, the site of an international high-diving tournament in July (www.marmeeting.com). A tiny beach at the bottom of the cleft, accessible by a stone staircase, is backed by a few abandoned houses. The main village is 300m above, in the upper Vallone del Furore. It sees few tourists at any time of the year, so it exudes a distinctly rural air despite the colourful murals and modern sculpture.

To get to upper Furore by car, follow the SS163 and then the SS366 signposts to Agerola.

Amalfi

☑089 / POP 5100

Amalfi's small size belies its past as a maritime superpower. Narrow alleys and steep staircases speak of the town's medieval history, and sunny piazzas overlook its small, pretty beach.

The town exudes history and culture, most notably in its over-sized Byzantine-influenced cathedral and diminutive Paper Museum. And while the permanent population is now a fairly modest 5000 or so, the numbers swell significantly during summer.

Just around the headland, neighbouring **Atrani** is a dense tangle of whitewashed alleys and arches centred on an agreeably lived-in piazza and small scimitar of beach; don't miss it.

◉ Sights & Activities

First stop is Piazza del Duomo, the town's focal-point square, with its majestic cathedral. To glean a sense of the town's medieval history, explore the narrow alleys parallel to the main street, with their steep stairways, covered porticos and historic shrine niches. Amalfi also has a beautiful seaside setting; it's the perfect spot for long, lingering lunches.

★ Cattedrale di Sant'Andrea
CATHEDRAL

(☑089 87 35 58; Piazza del Duomo; adult/reduced €3/1 between 10am-5pm; ◷7.30am-8.30pm, closed Nov-Mar) A melange of architectural styles, Amalfi's cathedral is a bricks-and-mortar reflection of the town's past as an 11th-century maritime superpower. It makes a striking impression at the top of a sweeping 62-step staircase. Between 10am and 5pm, the cathedral is only accessible through the adjacent Chiostro del Paradiso (p94), part of a four-section museum, incorporating the cloisters, the 9th-century Basilica del Crocefisso, the crypt of St Andrew and the cathedral itself. Outside these times, you can enter the cathedral for free.

The cathedral dates in part from the early 13th century. Its striped facade has been rebuilt twice, most recently at the end of the 19th century. It was constructed next to an older cathedral, the Basilica del Crocefisso, to which it long remained interconnected. The still-standing basilica now serves as a museum.

Amalfi

Amalfi

◉ Top Sights
1 Cattedrale di Sant'Andrea.................... C2

◉ Sights
Chiostro del Paradiso...................... (see 1)

🛏 Sleeping
2 Albergo Sant'Andrea............................ B2
3 DieciSedici.. D2

4 Hotel Centrale.. B2
5 Hotel Lidomare... B2
6 Residenza del Duca................................. B2

⊗ Eating
7 La Pansa...C2
8 Marina Grande..C3
9 Ristorante La Caravella...........................B2

The cathedral was originally built to house the relics of St Andrew the Apostle, which arrived here from Constantinople in 1208. Architecturally the building is a hybrid. The Sicilian Arabic-Norman style predominates outside, particularly in the two-tone masonry, mosaics and 13th-century bell tower. The huge bronze doors, the first of their type in Italy, were commissioned by a local noble and made in Syria before being shipped to Amalfi. The interior is primarily baroque with some fine statues at the altar, along with some interesting 12th- and 13th-century mosaics.

Chiostro del Paradiso   CHURCH
(☎089 87 13 24; Piazza del Duomo; adult/reduced €3/1; ⊗9am-7.45pm Jul-Aug, reduced hours Sep-early Jan & Mar-Jun, closed early Jan-Feb) To the left of Amalfi's cathedral porch, these magnificent Moorish-style

SENTIERO DEGLI DEI (WALK OF THE GODS)

The Sentiero degli Dei is the best-known walk on the Amalfi Coast for two reasons: first, it's spectacular from start to finish; and second, unlike most Amalfi treks, it doesn't need to involve inordinate amounts of stair-climbing. The walk starts in the village of **Bomerano** (a subdivision of Agerola), easily accessible from Amalfi town by SITA bus.

Beginning in the main square, where several cafes supply portable snacks, follow the red-and-white signs along Via Pennino. The start of the walk proper is marked by a **monument** inscribed with quotes by Italo Calvino and DH Lawrence. Views of terraced fields quickly open out as the path contours around a cliff-face and passes beneath the overhanging **Grotta del Biscotto** (Biscuit Cave). From here, the trail continues its traverse of the mountainside with some minor undulations. Periodically it dips into thickets of trees and sometimes you'll be required to negotiate rockier sections, but, in the main, the going is relatively easy.

The first main landmark after the Grotta is a path junction at **Colle Serra**. Here you get a choice between a low route or a high route. The low route is more exposed and threads its way through vineyards and rockier sections, with magnificent views of Praiano below. Roughly 800m along its course, it is possible to make a short diversion south to the **San Domenico Monastery**. The more popular high route (#327a) sticks to the rocky heights with broad, sweeping vistas. Both paths converge at a point called **Cisternulo**,

cloisters, complete with the remnants of 13th-century frescoes, were built in 1266 to house the tombs of Amalfi's prominent citizens; 120 marble columns support a series of tall, slender Arabic arches around a central garden. Entered from the cloisters, the **Basilica del Crocefisso** functions as a museum housing more frescoes and religious artefacts, including silver-embossed, 13th-century reliquary heads. Down below, the crypt contains the relics of St Andrew the Apostle.

Museo della Carta
MUSEUM

(Paper Museum; ☑089 830 45 61; www.museo dellacarta.it; Via delle Cartiere 23; adult/reduced €4/2.50; ⊙10am-6.30pm daily Mar-Oct, to 4pm Tue-Sun Nov-late Jan) Amalfi's Paper Museum is housed in a rugged, cave-like 13th-century paper mill (the oldest in Europe). It lovingly preserves the original paper presses, which are still in full working order, as you'll see during the 30-minute guided tour (in English). The tour explains the original cotton-based paper production and the subsequent wood-pulp manufacturing. Afterwards you might be inspired to pick up some of the stationery sold in the gift shop, including calligraphy sets and paper pressed with flowers.

Grotta dello Smeraldo
CAVE

(admission €5; ⊙9am-4pm) Four kilometres west of Amalfi, this grotto is named after the eerie emerald colour that emanates from the water. Stalactites hang down from the

24m-high ceiling, while stalagmites grow up to 10m tall. Buses regularly pass the car park above the cave entrance (from where you take a lift or stairs down to the rowing boats). Alternatively, **Coop Sant'Andrea** (☑089 87 31 90; www.coopsantandrea.com; Lungomare dei Cavalieri 1) runs boats from Amalfi (€10 return, plus cave admission). Allow 1½ hours for the return trip.

Amalfi Marine
BOATING

(☑338 3076125; www.amalfiboatrental.com; Spiaggia del Porto, Lungomare dei Cavalieri 7) Amalfi Marine hires out boats (without a skipper from €220 per day per boat excluding petrol; maximum six passengers). Private day-long tours with a skipper start from €600.

🛏 Sleeping

Despite its reputation as a day-trip destination, Amalfi has plenty of places to stay. It's not especially cheap, though, and most hotels are in the midrange to top-end price bracket. Always try to book ahead, as the summer months are very busy and many places close over winter. If you're coming by car, consider a hotel with a car park, as finding on-street parking can be especially painful.

Albergo Sant'Andrea
HOTEL €

(☑089 87 11 45; www.albergosantandrea.it; Salita Costanza d'Avalos 1; s/d €70/100; ⊙Mar-Dec; ❄☎) Enjoy the atmosphere of busy Piazza del Duomo from the comfort of your

1.5km further on. Just below Colle Serra, a path from the Sentiero degli Dei's alternative start in Praiano joins the main trail. Bear in mind that starting in Praiano involves a thigh-challenging climb up 1000 steps before you reach the trail proper.

After Cisternulo, the path kinks around some half-obscured *grotte* (caves) and descends into the Valle Grarelle before climbing back up to the finish point in the tiny village of **Nocelle**. A small kiosk selling cold drinks and coffee, served on a charming terrace, greets you as you enter the village. Alternatively, head a little further through the village to Piazza Santa Croce, where a stall dispenses freshly squeezed orange and lemon juice.

From here you have three options: 1) take stairs (around 1500 of them!) down through the village to be deposited on the coast road 2km east of Positano; 2) catch a bus from the end of Nocelle's one interconnecting road to Positano – small minibuses run by **Mobility Amalfi Coast** (☑ 089 81 30 77) depart 10 times a day; 3) a much nicer if longer option – especially if you're weary of steps at this point – is to continue along the path that leads west out of Nocelle towards Montepertuso. Don't miss the huge hole in the centre of the cliff at Montepertuso where it looks as though an irate giant has punched through the slab of limestone. In Montepertuso cut down past the church via a series of staircases to hit the northern fringes of Positano.

own room. This modest two-star has basic rooms with brightly coloured tiles and coordinating fabrics. Double glazing has helped cut down the piazza hubbub, which can reach fever pitch in high season – this is one place to ask for a room with a (cathedral) view.

★ DieciSedici B&B €€

(☑ 089 87 22 52; www.diecisedici.it; Piazza Municipio 10-16; d from €145; ☺ Mar-Oct; ❄) DieciSedici (1016) dresses up an old medieval palace in the kind of style that only the Italians can muster. The half-dozen rooms dazzle with chandeliers, mezzanine floors, glass balconies and gorgeous linens. Two rooms (the Junior Suite and Family Classic) come complete with kitchenettes. All have satellite TV, air-con and Bose sound systems.

Breakfast is laid on in a cafe in the nearby Piazza del Duomo.

Ercole di Amalfi Bed & Breakfast B&B €€

(☑ 089 83 18 43; www.ercolediamalfi.it; Via Giovanni d'Amalfi 2; d €160-190; ☺ year-round) You can catch a lemon on your breakfast plate at this hillside B&B on the road to Agerola, with a rustic terrace sheltered by trellises and fanned by sea breezes. Three stylish rooms feature vaulted ceilings, locally made tiles and swish modern bathrooms. It's a good spot for mountain strolls or peaceful contemplation. Note: there's a two-night minimum stay, but room rates drop significantly in quieter months (as low as €70).

Residenza del Duca HOTEL €€

(☑ 089 873 63 65; www.residencedelduca.it; Via Duca Mastalo II 3; d from €135; ☺ mid-Mar–Oct; ❄ ☎) This family-run hotel has just six rooms, all of them light, sunny and prettily furnished with antiques, majolica tiles and the odd chintzy cherub. The jacuzzi showers are excellent. Call ahead if you are carrying heavy bags, as it's a seriously puff-you-out staircase climb to reach here and a luggage service is included in the price.

Hotel Lidomare HOTEL €€

(☑ 089 87 13 32; www.lidomare.it; Largo Duchi Piccolomini 9; s/d €65/145; ❄ ☎) This gracious, old-fashioned, family-run hotel has no shortage of character. The large, luminous rooms have an air of gentility, with their appealingly haphazard decor, vintage tiles and fine antiques. Some have spa baths, others have sea views and a balcony, some have both. Rather unusually, breakfast is laid out on top of a grand piano.

Hotel Centrale HOTEL €€

(☑ 089 87 26 08; www.amalfihotelcentrale.it; Largo Duchi Piccolomini 1; d/tr/q €159/180/220; ☺ year-round; ❄ ☎) Central it is, with small, functional rooms berthed in a building accessed via a tiny little piazza in the *centro storico* (historic centre). The joy is not the rooms themselves (which are visually boring), but the window seat they offer over the buzzing Piazza del Duomo below. Be sure to ask for a front-facing room with a balcony.

ART IN A TOWER

Defensive towers sit all along the Amalfi Coast; ironically, they are generally known as Saracen towers, named after the very invaders they were erected to thwart. Although most lie empty, some are privately owned. At **Torre a Mare** (☎ 339 4401008; www.paolosandulli.com; Marina di Praia; ◷ 9am-1pm & 3.30-7pm) you can combine a visit to one such tower with enjoying the original sculptures and artwork of contemporary artist Paolo Sandulli. Most distinctive are his 'heads' with colourful sea-sponge hairdos. A spiral staircase leads to further works upstairs, including paintings.

Paolo's work is on display throughout the Amalfi Coast, including at Positano's prestigious Palazzo Murat (p87).

★ Hotel Santa Caterina   HOTEL €€€

(☎ 089 87 10 12; www.hotelsantacaterina.it; Strada Amalfitana 9; d €550-1300, ste from €2000; ◷ Mar-Oct; P ❄ 🛜 🏊) Worth perusing even if you're not staying here, if only to engage in a little Ferrari-spotting in the car park, the Santa Caterina is an Amalfi landmark and one of Italy's most famous hotels. Everything here oozes luxury, from the ultra-discreet service and fabulous gardens, to the private beach club and opulent rooms.

Hotel Luna Convento   HOTEL €€€

(☎ 089 87 10 02; www.lunahotel.it; Via Pantaleone Comite 33; d from €320; ◷ mid-Mar–Dec; P ❄ @ 🛜 🏊) This former convent was founded by St Francis in 1222 and has been a hotel for some 170 years. Rooms in the original building are in the former monks' cells, but there's nothing poky about the bright tiles, balconies and seamless sea views. The newer wing is equally beguiling, with religious frescoes over the beds. The cloistered courtyard is magnificent.

✕ Eating

Trattoria Il Mulino   ITALIAN €

(☎ 089 87 22 23; Via delle Cartiere 36; pizzas €6-11, meals €20-30; ◷ 11.30am-4pm & 6.30pm-midnight Tue-Sun) A TV-in-the-corner, kids-running-between-the-tables sort of place, this is about as authentic an eatery as you'll find in Amalfi. There are few surprises on the menu, just hearty, honest pastas, grilled meats and fish. For a taste of local seafood, try the octopus cake or pasta with swordfish. It's right at the top of the town under a simple plastic awning.

La Pansa   CAFE €

(☎ 089 87 10 65; www.pasticceriapansa.it; Piazza del Duomo 40; cornetti from €1, pastries from €1.80; ◷ 7.30am-midnight Wed-Mon, closed early Jan-early Feb) A marbled and mirrored fifth-generation cafe on Piazza del Duomo where black-bow-tied waiters serve minimalist Italian breakfasts: freshly made *cornetti* (croissants), full-bodied espresso and deliciously frothy cappuccino. Standout pastries include the crisp, flaky *coda di aragosta con crema di limone*, a lobster-tail-shaped concoction filled with a rich yet light lemon-custard cream.

Le Arcate   ITALIAN €€

(☎ 089 87 13 67; Largo Orlando Buonocore, Atrani; pizzas from €6, meals €30; ◷ 12.30-3.30pm & 7.30-11.30pm daily Jul & Aug, closed Mon Sep-Jun; ☎) If you've had it with the tourist tumult of Amalfi, try temporarily relocating to its quieter cousin Atrani to eat al fresco at one of its traditional restaurants. Le Arcate is right on the seafront with huge parasols shading its sprawl of tables, and a dining room in a stone-walled natural cave.

★ Ristorante La Caravella   ITALIAN €€€

(☎ 089 87 10 29; www.ristorantelacaravella.it; Via Matteo Camera 12; meals €50-90, tasting menus €50-135; ◷ noon-2.30pm & 7-11pm Wed-Mon; ❄) A restaurant of artists, art and artistry, Caravella once hosted Andy Warhol. No surprise that it doubles up as a de-facto gallery with frescoes, creative canvases and a ceramics collection. And then there's the food on the seven-course tasting menu, prepared by some of the finest culinary Caravaggios in Italy. Despite its fame, Michelin-starred Caravella, in business since 1959, remains an unpretentious and discreet place that's true to its seafood roots.

Not to be missed are the anchovy croquettes, fish with fennel and sun-dried tomatoes and – the *Mona Lisa* on the menu – a fine lemon soufflé. The wine list is, arguably, the best on the Amalfi Coast. Reservations essential.

Marina Grande   SEAFOOD €€€

(☎ 089 87 11 29; www.ristorantemarinagrande.com; Viale della Regione 4; meals €40-55; ◷ noon-3pm & 6.30-10.30pm Wed-Mon Mar-Oct; ☎) 🍃 Run by the same family for three generations, this savvy beachfront favourite serves fish so fresh it's almost flapping. It prides itself on the use of locally sourced organic produce, which, in Amalfi, means superlative amberjack, cuttlefish, prawns and mussels. Reservations are recommended.

ℹ Information

Tourist Office (☎089 87 11 07; www.amalfi touristoffice.it; Corso delle Repubbliche Marinare 27; ⊗8.30am-1pm & 2-6pm Mon-Sat Apr-Oct, 8.30am-1pm Mon-Sat Nov-Mar; 🐾) Just off the main seafront road in a small courtyard.

ℹ Getting There & Away

BOAT

The ferry terminal is a simple affair with several ticket offices located on the seafront.

CAR & MOTORCYCLE

Driving from the north, exit the A3 autostrada at Vietri sul Mare and follow the SS163. From the south, leave the A3 at Salerno and head for Vietri sul Mare and the SS163.

Parking

Parking is a problem in Amalfi, although there are some parking places on Piazza Flavio Gioia near the ferry terminal (€3 per hour), as well as at the underground car park Garage Luna Rossa (€2 to €4 per hour). The latter is accessed from the main seafront road between Amalfi and Atrani. From the car park, a pedestrian tunnel leads directly into the town.

Ravello

☑089 / POP 2490

Most people visit Ravello on a day trip from Amalfi – a nerve-tingling 7km drive up the Valle del Dragone – although, to best enjoy its romantic, otherworldly atmosphere, you'll need to stay here overnight. On Tuesday morning there's a lively street market in Piazza Duomo, where you'll find wine, mozzarella and olive oil, as well as discounted designer clothes.

◎ Sights

★ Villa Rufolo   GARDENS

(☑089 85 76 21; www.villarufolo.it; Piazza Duomo; adult/reduced €7/5; ⊗9am-9pm summer, reduced hours winter, tower museum 10am-7pm summer, reduced hours winter) To the south of Ravello's cathedral, a 14th-century tower marks the entrance to this villa, famed for its beautiful cascading gardens. Created by a Scotsman, Sir Francis Neville Reid, in 1853, they are truly magnificent, commanding divine panoramic views packed with exotic colours, artistically crumbling towers and luxurious blooms. Note that the gardens are at their best from May till October; they don't merit the entrance fee outside those times.

The villa was built in the 13th century for the wealthy Rufolo dynasty and was home to several popes as well as King Robert of Anjou. Wagner was so inspired by the gardens when he visited in 1880 that he modelled

Villa Rufolo

AMALFI COAST RAVELLO

Ravello

◉ Top Sights
1 Villa Rufolo A3

◎ Sights
2 Auditorium Oscar Niemeyer B2
3 Cathedral A3
4 Museo del Corallo Camo....................A3
5 Villa Cimbrone...................................A5

✚ Activities, Courses & Tours
6 Mamma Agata....................................A5

⊟ Sleeping
7 Albergo Ristorante Garden B3
8 Belmond Hotel Caruso.......................B2
9 Hotel Toro...A2
10 Palazzo Avino.....................................B2
11 Villa Casale...A3

✖ Eating
12 Babel..A3
13 Caffè Calce A3
14 Da Salvatore.......................................B3
15 Ristorante Pizzeria Vittoria A3

⊟ Shopping
16 Filo d'Autore A3
17 Profumi della Costiera A3

a British peer, Ernest Beckett, who reconfigured them with rose-beds, temples and a Moorish pavilion in the early 1900s.

The villa (also owned by Beckett) was something of a bohemian retreat in its early days; it was frequented by Greta Garbo and her lover Leopold Stokowski as a secret hideaway. Other illustrious former guests include Virginia Woolf, Winston Churchill, DH Lawrence and Salvador Dalí. The house and gardens sit atop a crag that's a 10-minute walk south of Piazza Duomo.

Cathedral   CATHEDRAL
(www.chiesaravello.com; Piazza Duomo; museum adult/reduced €3/1.50; ⊙8am-9pm) Forming the eastern flank of Piazza Duomo, Ravello's cathedral was built in 1086. Since that time it has undergone various makeovers. The facade is 16th century, but the central bronze door, one of only about two dozen in the country, dates from 1179. The interior is a late-20th-century interpretation of what the original must have once looked like.

Drawing it above the rank of a run-of-the-mill church is the striking pulpit, supported by six twisting columns set on marble lions and decorated with flamboyant mosaics of peacocks and other birds. Note also how the floor is tilted towards the square – a

the garden of Klingsor (the setting for the second act of the opera *Parsifal*) on them.

Villa Cimbrone   GARDENS
(☑089 85 74 59; www.hotelvillacimbrone.com/gardens; Via Santa Chiara 26; adult/reduced €7/4; ⊙9am-sunset) If you could bottle up a take-away image of the Amalfi, it might be the view from the **Belvedere of Infinity**, classical busts in the foreground, craggy coast splashed with pastel-shaded villages in the background. It's yours to admire at this re-fashioned 11th-century villa (now an upmarket hotel) with sublime gardens. Open to the public, the gardens were mainly created by

deliberate measure to enhance the perspective effect. The cathedral museum claims a modest collection of religious artefacts.

Auditorium Oscar Niemeyer THEATRE

(☎ 346 7378561; Via della Repubblica 12) Located just below the main approach to town, this modern building, which follows the natural slope of the hill, has caused a love-it-or-hate-it controversy in town. Designed by renowned Brazilian architect Oscar Niemeyer, it's characterised by the sinuous profile of a wave and approached via a rectangular exterior courtyard, which is typically the site of temporary exhibitions of world-class sculpture. The auditorium is a venue for concerts and exhibitions.

🍴 Courses

★ Mamma Agata COOKING

(☎ 089 85 70 19; www.mammaagata.com; Piazza San Cosma 9; courses €250) 🌿 The mamma of all cooking classes, this congenial family affair is famed for its private classes in the Agata home, producing simple, exceptional food using primarily organic ingredients. A one-day demonstration class culminates in an interlude on a lovely sea-view terrace, tasting what you've been taught to make and enjoying homemade *limoncello* (lemon liqueur). There is also a cookbook available for purchase. Course prices vary depending on the time of year.

🎆 Festivals & Events

Ravello's programme of classical music begins in late March and continues until late October. It reaches its crescendo in June and September with the International Piano Festival and Chamber Music Weeks. Performances by top Italian and international musicians are world-class, and the main venues are unforgettable. Tickets, bookable by phone or online, start at €27.50. For further information, contact the Ravello Concert Society (www.ravelloarts.org).

★ Ravello Festival PERFORMING ARTS

(☎ 089 85 84 22; www.ravellofestival.com; ⊙ Jul-Aug) In July and August, the Ravello Festival – established in 1953 – turns much of the town centre into a stage. Events range from orchestral concerts and chamber music to ballet performances, film screenings and exhibitions. The festival's most celebrated (and impressive) venue is the overhanging terrace in the Villa Rufolo gardens.

🛌 Sleeping

Ravello is an upmarket town and the accommodation reflects this, both in style and in price. There are some superb top-end hotels, several lovely midrange places and a fine *agriturismo* (farm stay) nearby. Book well ahead for summer – especially if you're planning to visit during the music festival.

Agriturismo Monte Brusara AGRITURISMO €

(☎ 089 85 74 67; www.montebrusara.com; Via Monte Brusara 32; d €94-100; ⊙ year-round; 🐾) 🌿 A working farm, this mountainside *agriturismo* is located a tough half-hour walk of about 1.5km from Ravello's centre (call ahead to arrange to be picked up). It's especially suited to families or those who simply want to escape the crowds and drink in the bucolic views.

Hotel Toro HOTEL €

(☎ 089 85 72 11; www.hoteltoro.it; Via Wagner 3; s/d from €56/82; ⊙ Easter-Nov; 🖧🐾) About as close as you can stay to Ravello's 'millionaires row' without being a millionaire, the Toro has been a hotel since the late 19th century; the Dutch artist MC Escher stayed in room 6 and was possibly inspired by the dizzily patterned tiles. Slightly dated rooms are decked out in traditional Amalfi style, with terracotta or marble tiles and cream furnishings.

Ravello Cathedral
MACIEJ MATLAK/SHUTTERSTOCK ©

CAMEO MUSEUM

Hidden away at the back of a cameo shop is the small **Museo del Corallo Camo** (📞 089 85 74 61; www.museodel corallo.com; Piazza Duomo 9, Ravello; ⏰ 10am-noon & 3-4pm Mon-Sat) with some magnificent pieces, including a mid-16th-century Madonna, Roman amphorae, early 19th-century tortoiseshell combs and some exquisite oil paintings. While Giorgio's cameos are beautiful (and popular with all kinds of well-known folk), you may think twice about the ethics of buying coral, especially the valuable red coral used locally. An intrinsic part of Mediterranean ecosystems, it is currently endangered due to commercial over-harvesting.

Villa Casale
APARTMENT €€

(📞 340 9479909; www.ravelloresidence.it; Via Orso Papice 4; apt €99-206, ste €179-280; ❄ 🤍 🌊) Practically next to the Villa Rufolo and enjoying the same glamorous view, Villa Casale consists of a handful of elegant suites and apartments arranged around a large pool. Top billing goes to the suites, graced with antiques and occupying the original 14th-century building. All the suites and apartments come with a self-contained kitchen and the property has tranquil terraced gardens.

Albergo Ristorante Garden
HOTEL €€

(📞 089 85 72 26; www.gardenravello.com; Via Giovanne Boccaccio 4; d €185-215; ⏰ mid-Mar–late Oct; ❄ 🤍 🌊) Still living off past glories (check out the 'celebs board' behind reception) the family-run Garden doesn't have to bend much with the times. Hoarding one of the best views on the Amalfi, no one really notices the nondescript but functional rooms. Throw in a decent restaurant (according to Gore Vidal) and a pool, and the word 'bargain' springs to mind.

Book early: it's mighty popular with the wedding set.

⭐ Belmond Hotel Caruso
HOTEL €€€

(📞 089 85 88 01; www.grandluxuryhotels.com; Piazza San Giovanni del Toro 2; d from €935; ⏰ mid-Apr–Oct; 🅿 ❄ 🤍 🌊) There can be no better place to swim than the Caruso's sensational infinity pool. Seemingly set on the edge of

a precipice, its blue waters merge with the sea and sky to magical effect. Inside, the sublimely restored 11th-century *palazzo* is no less impressive, with 15th-century vaulted ceilings, high-class ceramics and Moorish arches doubling as window frames.

⭐ Palazzo Avino
HOTEL €€€

(📞 089 81 81 81; www.palazzoavino.com; Via San Giovanni del Toro 28; d from €495; ⏰ Mar-Oct; ❄ 🤍 🌊) One of three luxury piles on Ravello's 'millionaires row', the erstwhile Palazzo Sasso has been a hotel on and off since 1880, sheltering many 20th-century luminaries – General Eisenhower planned the Allied attack on Monte Cassino here. Present-day guests prefer to recline more peacefully in their rooms amid hand-painted furniture, ornamented chaise lounges, fresh flowers and an original painting or two.

🍴 Eating

Babel
CAFE €

(📞 089 858 62 15; Via Trinità 13; meals €20; ⏰ 11.30am-5pm & 6.30-10.30pm daily May-Sep, closed Wed late Mar, Apr & Oct, closed Nov-late Mar; 🤍) A cool little deli-cafe with a compact menu of what you could call 'Italian tapas'. Affordable bites include Italian *gazpacho* (cold soup), bruschetta, dry polenta and creative salads with combos such as lemon and orange with goat's cheese and chestnut honey. It offers an excellent range of local wines, smooth jazz on the sound system, and Vietri-school ceramics for sale.

Caffè Calce
CAFE €

(📞 089 85 71 52; www.caffecalce.com; Viale Richard Wagner 3; gelato €2; ⏰ 8am-10pm) One in a quartet of refined cafes lined up al fresco in Ravello's Piazza Duomo, Calce supposedly serves the best coffee. You'll have to seek out its far crustier interior (on the corner by the Duomo) to peruse the pastry counter and the reliably good gelato.

⭐ Da Salvatore
ITALIAN €€

(📞 089 85 72 27; Via della Repubblica 2; meals €38-45, pizzas from €5; ⏰ 12.30-3pm & 7.30-10pm Tue-Sun Easter-Nov) Located just before the bus stop, Da Salvatore doesn't merely rest on the laurels of its spectacular terrace views. This is one of the coast's best restaurants, serving arresting dishes that showcase local produce with creativity, flair and whimsy; your premeal *benvenuto* (welcome) may include an *aperitivo* of Negroni encased in a white-chocolate ball.

Ristorante Pizzeria Vittoria
PIZZA €€

(📞089 85 79 47; www.ristorantepizzeriavittoria.it; Via dei Rufolo 3; pizza from €5, meals €30; ⏱12.15-3pm & 7.15-11pm; 🖼) Come here for exceptional pizza, with some 16 choices on the menu, including the Ravellese, with cherry tomatoes, mozzarella, basil and courgettes. Other dishes include grouper fish with creamed fennel and an innovative stuffed courgette-flower antipasto. The atmosphere is one of subdued elegance, with a small outside terrace and grainy historical pictures of Ravello on the walls.

Shopping

Profumi della Costiera
DRINKS

(📞089 85 81 67; www.profumidellacostiera.it; Via Trinità 37; ⏱9am-8pm) The *limoncello* produced here is made with local lemons; known to experts as *sfusato amalfitano*, they're enormous – about double the size of a standard lemon. The tot is made according to traditional recipes, so there are no preservatives and no colouring. All bottles carry the IGP (Indicazione Geografica Proteta; Protected Geographical Indication) quality mark. You may see the bottling process in progress when you visit; it takes place at the back of the shop.

Filo d'Autore
CLOTHING

(📞089 85 84 67; www.filodautoreravello.it; Via Trinità 8; scarves from €35; ⏱9.30am-9pm) Although you may associate cashmere with more northern climes, this tiny shop in the Ravello backstreets is worth a visit to view the exceptional quality of the locally produced clothing, made primarily from pure cashmere, as well as linen.

ℹ Information

Tourist Office (📞089 85 70 96; www.ravellotime.it; Piazza Fontana Moresca 10; ⏱9am-7pm summer, to 5pm rest of year) Shares digs with the police station. Provides brochures and maps, and can also assist with accommodation.

ℹ Getting There & Away

From the bus stop on the eastern side of Amalfi's Piazza Flavio Gioia, SITA Sud (p92) runs up to 27 buses daily to Ravello (€1.30, 25 minutes).

Minori

About 3.5km east of Amalfi, or a steep 45-minute walk down from Ravello, Minori is a small, workaday town, popular with holidaying Italians. Much scruffier than its refined coastal cousins Amalfi and Positano, it's no less dependent on tourism yet seems more genuine, with its festive seafront, pleasant beach, atmospheric pedestrian shopping streets and noisy traffic jams. The town is also known for its history of pasta making, dating back to medieval times; its speciality is *scialatielli* (thick ribbons of fresh pasta), featured on many local restaurant menus.

Villa Romana Antiquarium (p102)

Ceramics for sale, Vietri sul Mare

Villa Romana Antiquarium
HISTORIC BUILDING

(☑089 85 28 93; Via Capodipiazza 28; ⊙8am-7pm) FREE Rediscovered in the 1930s, the 1st-century Villa Romana Antiquarium is a typical example of the splendid homes that Roman nobles built as holiday retreats in the period before Mt Vesuvius' AD 79 eruption. The best-preserved rooms surround the garden on the lower level, the highlight being a floor mosaic depicting a bull. There's also a slightly tatty museum exhibiting various artefacts, including a collection of 6th-century-BC to 6th-century-AD amphorae.

Gusta Minori
FOOD FESTIVAL

(www.gustaminori.it; ⊙early Sep) Food lovers on the coast gather in Minori for the town's annual food jamboree, with pasta stalls (and the like) as well as live music and other cultural events.

★ Sal de Riso
DESSERTS €

(☑089 87 79 41; www.salderiso.it; Via Roma 80; desserts from €4.50; ⊙7am-1am) *Pasticceria*? Yes. Cafe? Yes. Gelateria? Yes. Sal de Riso is all these things and more: an emporium of edible sweetness that will make your eyes pop out and your blood sugar shoot up in the same bite. The ample glass display cases are like an art gallery of avant-garde desserts crammed with delicate cheesecakes, eclairs, sponges and pastries.

Il Giardiniello
ITALIAN €€

(☑089 87 70 50; www.ristorantegiardiniello.com; Corso Vittorio Emanuele 17; pizza from €8, meals €35-48; ⊙12.20-2.30pm & 6.30-11.30pm Thu-Tue) The old sage of Minori restaurants has been around as long as the Fiat Cinquecento and is arguably just as good. Sit on the terrace underneath a canopy of fragrant jasmine and enjoy highbrow, art-on-a-plate dishes that revolve around seafood, with a surprise inclusion of rabbit served with bacon and black truffles.

🛈 Information

Tourist Office (☑089 87 70 87; www.proloco.minori.sa.it; Via Roma 32; ⊙8.30am-1pm & 4-8pm Mon-Sat, 8.30am-1pm Sun) Head to this small office on the seafront for general information and walking maps.

Cetara
POP 2140

Just beyond Erchie and its pleasant beach, Cetara is an important fishing centre. Recently, locals have resurrected the production of what is known as *colatura di alici,* a strong anchovy essence believed to be the descendant of garum, the Roman fish seasoning.

Sagra del Tonno
FOOD FESTIVAL

(⊙late Jul/early Aug) Each year the village celebrates *sagra del tonno,* a festival dedicated to tuna and anchovies. If you can time your visit accordingly, there are plenty of opportunities for tasting, as well as music and other general festivities. Further details are available from the tourist office.

B&B Mara
B&B €
(☑089 26 18 96; www.bbmara.com; Parco degli Ulivi 3; r €60-70) For a quiet, private and very comfortable B&B with a full-on Cetarese flavour, opt for Mara's place, a sparkling and characterful little abode located in an otherwise unremarkable apartment building perched high above Cetara's fishing harbour. Two of the three large, sunny rooms have balconies, and all have vivid splashes of colour plus fridges stocked with beer and soft drinks. Mara and her nonna are wonderful, hands-on hosts.

Cetara Punto e Pasta
CAMPANIAN €€
(☑089 26 11 09; Corso Garibaldi 14; meals €25; ⊙noon-4pm & 7-11.30pm Mon, Wed, Thu & Sun, 11.30am-midnight Fri & Sat) This tiny eating joint is barely larger than a studio flat, with six tables and an open kitchen from which the industrious owner-chef performs minor miracles with local fish and homemade pasta. The menu is scrawled on a blackboard. Don't leave before tasting the fresh-off-the-boat *colatura di alici,* made with anchovies.

Ristorante e Pizzeria da Spadone
CAMPANIAN €€
(☑089 26 12 46; Corso Garibaldi 5; meals €23-28; ⊙noon-3.30pm & 7pm-midnight) Spadone is the kind of place where the head chef stands ingratiatingly at the front door at 7pm, smudges of pizza flour still stuck to his apron. Come here for simple renditions of age-old recipes done well – the *linguine alla vongole* (linguine with clams), pizza and fried anchovies are all good. Desserts come from the delectable Sal de Riso in nearby Minori.

ℹ Information

Tourist Office (☑089 26 17 01; Piazza San Francesco 15; ⊙9am-1pm & 5pm-midnight) The local Pro Loco has a good town map with walking trails. Staff might only speak Italian.

Vietri sul Mare

Marking the end of Amalfi's coastal road, Vietri sul Mare is the ceramics capital of Campania. Production dates back to Roman times, but it took off on an industrial scale in the 16th and 17th centuries with the development of high, three-level furnaces. The unmistakable local style – bold brush strokes and strong Mediterranean colours – found favour in the royal court of Naples, which became one of Vietri's major clients. Later, in the 1920s and '30s, the arrival of international artists (mainly Germans) led to a shake-up of traditional designs. These days, the *centro storico* is packed with decorative tiled-front shops selling ceramic wares of every description.

Museo della Ceramica
MUSEUM
(☑089 21 18 35; Villa Guariglia, Via Nuova Raito; ⊙9am-3pm Tue-Sat, 9.30am-1pm Sun) FREE For a primer on Vietri's ceramics past, head to this museum in the nearby village of Raito. Housed in a mildewed villa surrounded by a park, the museum has a comprehensive collection, including pieces from the 'German period' (1929–47).

Ceramica Artistica Solimene
CERAMICS
(☑089 21 02 43; www.ceramicasolimene.it; Via Madonna degli Angeli 7; ⊙9am-8pm Mon-Fri, 9am-1.30pm & 4-8pm Sat, 9am-1.30pm & 4-7pm Sun) This vast factory outlet, which looks like something Gaudí might have built, is the most famous ceramics shop in town. It sells everything from egg cups to ornamental mermaids. Even if you don't go in, it's worth having a look at the shop's extraordinary glass-and-ceramic facade. It was designed by Italian architect Paolo Soleri, who studied under Frank Lloyd Wright.

ℹ Information

Tourist Office (☑089 21 12 85; www.proloco vietrisulmare.it; Via San Giovanni; ⊙9.30am-12.30pm Mon, Wed & Fri) This moderately helpful office with limited hours is next to the *duomo.*

Salerno & the Cilento

Don't miss the Cilento region, one of this area's lesser-known glories, with a largely undeveloped coastal strip and a beautiful national park famed for its orchids.

Salerno

📱 089 / POP 133,970

Upstaged by the postcard-pretty towns along the Amalfi Coast, Campania's second-largest city is a pleasant surprise. A decade of civic determination has turned this major port into one of southern Italy's most liveable cities, and its small but buzzing historic centre is a vibrant mix of medieval churches, tasty trattorias and good-spirited, bar-hopping locals.

🅞 Sights

★ **Duomo**   CATHEDRAL

(📱 089 23 13 87; www.cattedraledisalerno.it; Piazza Alfano; ⊗ 8.30am-8pm Mon-Sat, 8.30am-1pm & 4-8pm Sun) One of Campania's strangely under-the-radar sights, Salerno's impressive cathedral is considered by aficionados to be the most beautiful medieval church in Italy. Built by the Normans in the 11th century and later aesthetically remodelled in the 18th century, it sustained severe damage in a 1980 earthquake. It is dedicated to San Matteo (St Matthew), whose remains were reputedly brought to the city in 954 and now lie beneath the main altar in the vaulted crypt.

Take special note of the magnificent main entrance, the 12th-century **Porta dei Leoni**, named after the marble lions at the foot of the stairway. It leads through to a beautiful, harmonious courtyard, surrounded by graceful arches and overlooked by a 12th-century bell tower. Carry on through the huge bronze doors (similarly guarded by lions), which were cast in Constantinople in the 11th century. When you come to the three-aisled interior, you will see that it is largely baroque, with only a few traces of the original church. These include parts of the transept and choir floor and the two raised pulpits in front of the choir stalls. Throughout the church you can see highly detailed 13th-century mosaic work redolent of the extraordinary early-Christian mosaics in Ravenna.

PLAN YOUR ROUTE

3 **Southern Larder** (p37) Passing through Salerno on the way to Paestum, this trip explores Campania's raw beauty.

4 **Cilento Coastal Trail** (p45) From Paestum to Sapri, this rugged coastline boasts fascinating hilltop towns and ancient Greek ruins.

SWEET TREAT

Look for *torta ricotta e pera* (ricotta and pear tart), a speciality in Salerno and sold throughout the Cilento region. Just about every *pasticceria* (pastry shop) sells this delicious sweet and fruity delicacy – although it's the locals' favourite as well, so it tends to sell out fast.

In the right-hand apse, don't miss the **Cappella delle Crociate** (Chapel of the Crusades), containing powerful frescoes and more wonderful mosaics. It was so named because crusaders' weapons were blessed here. Under the altar stands the tomb of 11th-century pope Gregory VII.

Museo Archeologico Provinciale   MUSEUM
(☑ 089 23 11 35; www.museoarcheologicosalerno.it; Via San Benedetto 28; adult/reduced €4/2; ⊙ 9am-7.30pm Tue-Sun) The province's restored and revitalised main archaeological museum is an excellent showcase for the excavated history of the surrounding area, dating back to cave dwellers and the colonising Greeks. The pièce de résistance is the 1st-century-BC *Testa bronzea di Apollo* (Bronze head of Apollo). Showcased in its own small room upstairs, the head is thought to have been part of a larger statue; it was found by a fisherman in the Gulf of Salerno in 1930.

Castello di Arechi   CASTLE
(☑ 089 296 40 15; www.ilcastellodiarechi.it; Via Benedetto Croce; adult/reduced €4/2; ⊙ 9am-5pm Tue-Sat, to 3.30pm Sun) Hop on bus 19 from Piazza XXIV Maggio to visit Salerno's most famous landmark, the forbidding Castello di Arechi, dramatically positioned 263m above the city. Originally a Byzantine fort, it was built by the Lombard duke of Benevento, Arechi II, in the 8th century and subsequently modified by the Normans and Aragonese, most recently in the 16th century.

Museo Virtuale della Scuola Medica Salernitana   MUSEUM
(☑ 089 257 32 13; www.museovirtualescuolamedica salernitana.beniculturali.it; Via Mercanti 74; adult/reduced €3/2; ⊙ 9am-1.30pm Tue-Sun mid-Oct–Jun, 9am-1.30pm Mon-Sat Jul–mid-Oct; ⊕) In Salerno's historic centre, this small, slightly forlorn museum deploys videos and touchscreen technology to explore the teachings and wince-inducing procedures of Salerno's once-famous, now-defunct medical institute.

Established around the 9th century, the school was the most important centre of medical knowledge in medieval Europe, reaching the height of its prestige in the 11th century. It was closed in the early 19th century.

🛌 Sleeping

The little accommodation that Salerno offers is fairly uninspiring, although, conveniently, there are several reasonable hotels in the town centre. Prices tend to be considerably lower than on the Amalfi Coast.

Ostello Ave Gratia Plena   HOSTEL €
(☑ 089 23 47 76; www.ostellodisalerno.it; Via dei Canali; dm/s/d €16/45/65; @ 🗺) Housed in a 16th-century convent, Salerno's excellent HI hostel is right in the heart of the *centro storico* action. Inside, there's a charming central courtyard and a range of bright rooms, from dorms to great-bargain doubles with private bathroom.

Hotel Montestella   HOTEL €€
(☑ 089 22 51 22; www.hotelmontestella.it; Corso Vittorio Emanuele II 156; d €90-125, tr €95-160; ✳ @ 🗺) Within walking distance of just about anywhere worth going to, the modern, if slightly bland, Montestella is on Salerno's main pedestrian thoroughfare, halfway between the *centro storico* and the train station. Although some rooms are quite small, all are light and contemporary, with firm beds and patterned feature walls.

Museo Archeologico Provinciale
LUCAMATO/SHUTTERSTOCK ©

400 m
0.2 miles

G1
G2
G3
G4

Irno

Via Torrione

A3 (Southbound);
Paestum (36km)

Lungomare Guglielmo Marconi

Via Dalmazia

Bus
Station

Piazza
Vittorio
Veneto

Busitalia
Campania

Piazza
Giuseppe
Mazzini

Curcio Viaggi

Piazza della
Concordia

F1 F2 F3 F4

Via Nizza

Corso Garibaldi

Porto Turistico
Ferry & Hydrofoil
Terminal

E1 E2 E3 E4

Via Volpe

Castello di Arechi
(4km)

Piazza
XXIV
Maggio

Corso Vittorio Emanuele II

Via Diaz

Via Cilento

Lungomare Trieste

4

D1 D2 D3 D4

Via San Benedetto

Via Vella

Via Iannelli

Via Roma

2

Gulf of Salerno
(Golfo di Salerno)

C1 C2 C3 C4

Piazza
Alfano

Duomo
1

Via S.Michele

6

3

Via Mercanti

Via Duomo

B1 B2 B3 B4

Via del Canali

5
7

Vicolo della
Neve

9

A1 A2 A3 A4

Piazza
Sedile del
Campo

8

Piazza
Amendola

Amalfi (26km);
Positano (42km)

Molo
Manfredi

Salerno

 **Eating**

Mariterraneo   MEDITERRANEAN €€

(☎089 943 31 38; Vico Grimoaldo 12; meals €35-40; ☺6-11pm Tue-Sat, 11.30am-2.30pm Sun) Hard to find, this new purveyor of Slow Food shines brightly amid the grubby graffiti, drying washing and overflowing bins of the *centro storico*. The artistically presented food will have you unashamedly reaching for your camera – if you can put off eating it for that long. Try the delicately baked fish nestled on a bed of vegetables.

Cicirinella   ITALIAN €€

(☎089 22 65 61; Via Genovesi 28; meals €25; ☺8pm-midnight daily, 1-3pm Sat & Sun; 🕿) This place, tucked behind the cathedral, has that winning combination of an earthy and inviting atmosphere and unfailingly good, delicately composed dishes. Exposed stone, shelves of wine and an open-plan kitchen set the scene for traditional Campanian cuisine like pasta with seafood and chickpeas, or a mussel soup that tastes satisfyingly of the sea.

Sant'Andrea   ITALIAN €€

(☎328 727274; www.ristorantesantandrea.it; Piazza Sedile del Campo 58; pizzas €4-6, meals €25-30; ☺12.30-3pm & 8pm-midnight Tue-Sun; 🕿) There's an earthy southern-Italian flavour at this classic old-town trattoria, with its terrace surrounded by historic houses decorated with last night's pajamas hung out to dry. Choices are more innovative than you would expect, and include such seafood dishes as squid with porcini mushrooms and cuttlefish with creamed vegetables.

Vicolo della Neve   ITALIAN €€

(☎089 22 57 05; Vicolo della Neve 24; meals €22-30; ☺7.15pm-midnight Mon, Tue & Thu-Sat, 12.30-3.30pm Sun) A city institution on a scruffy street, this is the archetypal *centro storico* trattoria, with brick arches, fake frescoes and walls hung with works by local artists. The menu is unwaveringly authentic, with pizzas, calzoni, *peperoni ripieni* (stuffed peppers) and a top-notch *parmigiana di melanzane* (baked eggplant). It can get incredibly busy: book in advance, especially later in the week.

ℹ Information

Tourist Office (☎089 23 14 32; Lungomare Trieste 7; ☺9am-7pm Mon-Sat) Located right on the promenade. Has limited information.

ℹ Getting There & Away

Salerno is on the A3 between Naples and Reggio di Calabria; the A3 is toll-free from Salerno south. Take the Salerno exit and follow signs to the *centro* (city centre). If you want to hire a car, there's a **Europcar** (☎089 258 07 75; www.europcar.com; Via Clemente Mauro 18; ☺8.30am-1pm & 2.30-6.30pm Mon-Fri, 8.30am-1pm Sat) agency not far from the train station.

Paestum

Paestum, or Poseidonia as the city was originally called (in honour of Poseidon, the Greek god of the sea), was founded in the 6th century BC by Greek settlers and fell under Roman control in 273 BC. Decline later set in following the demise of the Roman Empire. Savage raids by the Saracens and periodic outbreaks of malaria forced the steadily dwindling population to abandon the city altogether. Although most people visit Paestum for the day, there is a surprising number of good hotels, and this delightful rural area makes a convenient stopover point for travellers heading for the Cilento region.

★ Casale Giancesare
Villa Agricola   B&B €

(☎0828 199 96 14; www.casalegiancesare.com/en; Via Giancesare 8, Capaccio Paestum; s €50-120, d €60-150, 4-person apt from €80-185; P✳@ 🕿🗋) A 19th-century former farmhouse, this elegantly decorated, stone-clad B&B is run by the delightful Voza family, who will happily ply you with their homemade wine,

PAESTUM'S TEMPLES

Very different to Pompeii, Paestum's **temples** (Area Archeologica di Paestum; ☑ 0828 81 10 23; www.museopaestum.beniculturali.it; adult/reduced incl museum €12/2, ruins only €8/2; ⊙ 8.30am-7.30pm daily, last entry 6.50pm, museum closed Mon) are smaller, older, more Greek and – crucially – a lot less overrun. Consequently, it is possible to steal some reflective moments here as the sun slants across the giant Doric columns of this once great city of Magna Graecia (the Greek colony that once covered much of southern Italy). Take the train to Paestum station. Buy your tickets in the museum, just east of the site, before entering from the main entrance at the northern end.

Paestum was probably founded by Greeks from Sybaris in the 6th century BC. It later became a Roman city, but was abandoned in the Middle Ages. The ruins were rediscovered in the 1760s, but not fully unearthed and excavated until the 1950s.

The first structure is the 6th-century-BC **Tempio di Cerere** (Temple of Ceres); originally dedicated to Athena, it served as a Christian church in medieval times.

As you head south, you can pick out the basic outline of the large rectangular forum, the heart of the ancient city. Among the partially standing buildings are the vast domestic housing area and, further south, the amphitheatre. Both provide evocative glimpses of daily life here in Roman times. In the former houses you'll see mosaic floors, and a marble *impluvium* (cistern) that stood in the atrium and collected rainwater.

The **Tempio di Nettuno** (Temple of Neptune), dating from about 450 BC, is the largest and best preserved of the three temples at Paestum; only parts of its inside walls and roof are missing. The two rows of double-storied columns originally divided the outer colonnade from the *cella,* or inner chamber, where a statue of the temple deity would have been displayed. Despite its commonly used name, many scholars believe that the temple was actually dedicated to the Greek goddess Hera, sister and wife of Greek god Zeus.

Almost next door, the so-called **basilica** (a temple to the goddess Hera) is Paestum's oldest surviving monument. Dating from the middle of the 6th century BC, it's a magnificent sight, with nine columns across and 18 along the sides. Ask someone to take your photo next to one of the columns: it's a good way to appreciate the scale.

Save time for the **museum** (☑ 0828 81 10 23; adult/reduced incl temples €9.50/4.75; ⊙ 8.30am-7.30pm, last entry 6.50pm, closes 1.40pm 1st & 3rd Mon of month), which covers two floors and houses a collection of interesting bas-relief friezes, plus numerous frescoes dating back to the 5th century BC.

The archaeological site and adjoining museum are particularly evocative in spring when they are surrounded by scarlet poppies.

limoncello and marmalades; they even make their own olive oil. The B&B is located 2.5km from Paestum and is surrounded by vineyards and olive and mulberry trees; views are marvellous, particularly from the swimming pool.

Casa Rubini   INN €

(☑ 0828 199 22 55; www.casarubini.it; Via Tavernelle 5; d €58-70; P 🖵) So authentically 'olde' is this rustic inn within sight of the Paestum ruins, you can almost imagine that Da Vinci was a recent guest. Attic-like rooms come with sloping ceilings, exposed stone walls, fat wooden beams and Dante quotes emblazoned on the paintwork, plus there's a wonderful adjoining bar/restaurant where local troubadours (singing guitar players) often drop by.

Nonna Sceppa   ITALIAN €€

(☑ 0828 85 10 64; Via Laura 53; meals €35; ⊙ 12.30-3pm & 7.30-11pm Fri-Wed; 🖵 🖵) Seek out the superbly prepared, robust dishes at Nonna Sceppa, a family-friendly restaurant that's gaining a reputation throughout the region for excellence. Dishes are firmly seasonal and, during summer, concentrate on fresh seafood, like the refreshingly simple grilled fish with lemon. Other popular choices include risotto with zucchini and artichokes, and spaghetti with lobster.

❶ Information

Tourist Office (☑ 0828 81 10 16; www. infopaestum.it; Via Magna Grecia 887; ⊙ 9am-1pm & 2-4pm) Across the street from the archaeological site, this helpful tourist office offers a map of the site, as well as information on the greater Cilento region.

Agropoli

Located just south of Paestum, Agropoli is a busy summer resort but otherwise a pleasant, tranquil town that is a good base for exploring Cilento's coastline and national park. While the shell is a fairly faceless grid of shop-lined streets, the kernel – the historic city centre – is a fascinating tangle of narrow cobbled streets with ancient churches, venerable residents and a castle with superb views.

The town has been inhabited since Neolithic times, with later inhabitants including the Greeks, the Romans, the Byzantines and the Saracens. In 915 Agropoli fell under the jurisdiction of the bishops and was subsequently ruled by feudal lords. It was a target of raids from North Africa in the 16th and 17th centuries, when the population dwindled to just a few hundred. Today it's the largest and most vibrant town along the Cilento coast.

🔴 Sights & Activities

To reach the *centro storico*, head for Piazza Veneto Victoria, the pedestrian-only part of the modern town, where cafes and gelaterie are interspersed with plenty of shopping choice. Head up Corso Garibaldi and take the wide Ennio Balbo Scaloni steps until you reach the fortified *borgo* (medieval hamlet). Follow the signs to the castle.

Il Castello   CASTLE
(📞 0974 82 74 07; ⏰ 8am-10pm Jul-Sep) `FREE`
Built by the Byzantines in the 5th century, the castle was strengthened during the Angevin period, the time of the War of the Vespers, which was initially sparked by an uprising in Sicily during evening prayers. Agropoli's castle continued to be modified, and only part of the original defensive wall remains. It's an enjoyable walk here from Agropoli's historic centre, and you can wander the ramparts and drink in magnificent views of the coastline and town.

Cilento Sub Diving Center   DIVING
(📞 338 2374603; Via San Francesco 30; dives from €50) Indulge in your favourite watery pursuit here. Courses include snorkelling for beginners, open-water junior dives (from 12 years) and wreck diving; the latter includes the harrowing viewing of the hulks of ships, tanks and planes that were famously destroyed in the region during WWII. Diving sites include such tantalising areas as the

waters off the coast at Paestum, where – who knows? – you may just come across your very own bronze Apollo.

🛏️ Sleeping & Eating

B&B I Delfini   B&B €
(📞 339 3095895; www.idelfinibb.com; Via Toscanini 9; s/d €40/75; ❄️ 📶) A clean, economical and modern B&B close to the centre of Agropoli. It is run by the affable Alfonso who is a mine of information on the local sights and very generous with his time. Rooms have new bathrooms, large towels and pleasant Agropoli motifs emblazoned on the walls. A veritable bargain at the price.

Hotel Serenella   HOTEL €
(📞 0974 82 33 33; www.hotelserenella.it; Via San Marco 140; s/d €54/90; 🅿️ ❄️ 📶) Gleaming white Serenella is about as posh as Agropoli gets. It's right on the seafront (good start) and has an alluring lounge bar out the front (another plus). The rooms, though plain, are large and don't lack anything except perhaps a bit of character. Bonuses are free parking, private beach access and half- and full-board rates.

⭐ Pecora Nera   PIZZA €
(📞 320 6115112; Piazza della Mercanzia; pizzas €5-12; ⏰ 7:30pm-1am) Agropoli's self-proclaimed 'black sheep', Pecora Nera has emerged as a new challenger for the title of the town's 'best pizza' and they might just be on to something. The small but slickly furnished pizzeria in a piazza by the port is run by a hip team of *ragazzi* (guys) whose uncluttered pizzas use a light chewy dough and carefully sourced DOP ingredients.

Anna   PIZZA €
(📞 0974 82 37 63; www.ristorantepizzeriaanna.it; Via San Marco 32; pizzas from €3.50, meals from €18; ⏰ noon-3pm & 7pm-midnight) At the city-centre end of the promenade, no-fuss Anna has been a local favourite for decades. Family-run, with a B&B upstairs, it's best known for its pizzas, with expert bases made either with standard, wholewheat, spelt or *kamut* (Khorasan wheat) flour. Try the *sorpresa* pizza, whose eight-slice selection includes mussels, aubergines, courgettes, marinated pork, ham, prawns and spicy sausage.

ℹ️ Information

Tourist Office (📞 0974 82 74 71; Viale Europa 34; ⏰ 9.30am-2pm) Dispatching basic information out of a small kiosk in the town centre.

THE MEDITERRANEAN DIET

Named an intangible cultural heritage by Unesco in 2013, the Mediterranean diet has long been held up as an elixir of good health, neighbourliness and sustainable living. One of its first advocates was American medical researcher Dr Ancel Keys (1904–2004) who launched his famous study concerning the health benefits of the Mediterranean diet in the 1950s using research gleaned, in part, from Italy's Cilento coast, in particular the village of **Pioppi**. Of the residents of Pioppi, Keys famously noted that the people were older and more energetic thanks to regular physical activity and a working life that revolved around tending crops on the hillsides and rowing fishing boats across the bay.

Keys was struck by the low rate of heart disease among poor people here, compared to the rate among well-fed northern Europeans and Americans. He himself adopted the Mediterranean diet and moved to Pioppi, where he lived to be 100 years old.

More recently the focus has switched 7km west to the similarly small village of Acciaroli when it was discovered that one in ten of the population of around 650 was over 100 years old. In 2016, medical researchers from the US and Italy spent six months studying Acciaroli's residents' longevity, concluding that the village's seniors had abnormally good blood circulation, along with low incidences of diabetes, heart disease, cataracts and dementia. The reasons for the trend are still not fully understood, but many scientists have attributed it to a mixture of genetics and diet – Acciaroli's residents are particularly partial to anchovies, olive oil, wine and herbs, most notably rosemary.

Cilento Coast

While the Cilento stretch of coastline lacks the gloss and sophistication of the Amalfi Coast, it can afford to have a slight air of superiority when it comes to its beaches: a combination of secluded coves and long stretches of golden sand with a welcome lack of overpriced ice creams and sunbeds. Beyond the options outlined below, the far-southeastern stop along the coastline is Sapri, which has two pleasant beaches in the centre of town.

Agropoli to Castellabate

Around 14km south of Agropoli is the former fishing village of **Santa Maria di Castellabate**. Santa Maria's golden sandy beach stretches for around 4km, which equals plenty of towel space on the sand, even in midsummer.

Approaching from its coastal sidekick, Santa Maria de Castellabate, the summit of **Castellabate** is marked by the broad Belvedere di San Costabile, from where there are sweeping coastal views. Flanking this are the shell of a 12th-century castle, with only the defensive walls still standing, and an art gallery. The surrounding labyrinth of narrow pedestrian streets is punctuated by ancient archways, small piazzas and the occasional

palazzo (mansion). The animated heart and soul of town is the numerological mouthful Piazza 10 Ottobre 1123, with its panoramic views of the Valle dell'Annunziata.

San Marco di Castellabate to Acciaroli

Heading south from Castellabate, the next stop is the pretty little harbour at **San Marco di Castellabate**, overlooked by the handsome, ivy-clad Approdo hotel. This was once an important Greek and Roman port, and tombs and other relics have been discovered that are now on view in the museum at Paestum. The area between Santa Maria di Castellabate and San Marco is popular for diving. San Marco's blue-flag beach is a continuation of the sandy stretch from Santa Maria di Castellabate.

The coastal road heading south lacks the drama (views and traffic) of its Amalfi counterpart but is still prettily panoramic. It's an area that Ernest Hemingway apparently rated highly, particularly **Acciaroli**, which – despite the disquieting amount of surrounding concrete – has a charming centre. Head for the sea and the peeling facade of the Parrocchia di Acciaroli church, with its abstract 1920s stained-glass windows. The surrounding streets and piazzas have been tastefully restored using local stone and traditional architecture, and the cafes, bars and restaurants have a buzzing, fashionable appeal.

Pioppi to Pisciotta

A short 10km hop south of Acciaroli is tiny picturesque Pioppi, with its pristine pebble beach and handful of shops and restaurants.

Next stop is **Marina di Casal Velino**, which features a small, pretty harbour and a family-style stretch of sand, complete with plenty of ice-cream opportunities, a playground and pedal boats.

Continuing southeast, **Ascea** – best known as the home of philosophers Parmenides and Zeno of Elea, as well as the famous Eleatic School of Philosophy – boasts some impressive Greek ruins. Fronted by 5km of glorious sandy beach, the town is wonderful for a dip.

Further on, lovely **Pisciotta** is a medieval town piled high above a ridge. Head straight for the central Piazza Raffaele Pinto, its terraced bars and benches occupied by robust elderly locals. There are a couple of excellent restaurants in town and one of the region's top boutique hotels. Be sure to stop by the Marina di Pisciotta, lined with seafood restaurants and cafes. Carry on to the far end of the promenade and take a look at the stones and pebbles on the beach, fabulously patterned and in all shades of mauve, grey, cream and ochre.

 **Sights**

Parco Archeologico di Elea Velia   ARCHAEOLOGICAL SITE
See p50

 **Sleeping**

⭐ **Marulivo Hotel**   BOUTIQUE HOTEL €€
(☏ 0974 97 37 92; www.marulivohotel.it; Via Castello, Pisciotta; d €70-140, ste €130-220; ☺ Easter-Oct; ❄ 📶) *The* hotel in tiny Pisciotta is a sublime place: a beautifully restored 14th-century monastery daubed with elegant antique touches and crowned with a wisteria-flecked terrace. Great for romance, the 11 handsome rooms feature earthy colours, carefully chosen furnishings, crisp white linen and exposed stone walls. The owners love their village and their enthusiasm is contagious.

Residenza d'Epoca 1861   GUESTHOUSE €€
(☏ 0974 96 14 54; www.residenzadepoca1861.it; Lungomare Perrotti, Santa Maria di Castellabate; d €130-160, ste €170; ❄ 📶) Occupying an 18th-century mansion on Santa Maria di Castellabate's historic waterfront, this small, impeccably run guesthouse offers sea views from every room, plus creamy white interiors with discreet splashes of modernist colour. There's an affiliated restaurant called Osteria 1861.

ROBERTO LO SAVIO/EYEEM/GETTY IMAGES ©

Pisciotta

Marulivo Hotel (p111)

Villa Sirio
HOTEL €€€

(☎0974 96 10 99; www.villasirio.it; Via Lungomare de Simone 15, Santa Maria di Castellabate; d €215-260; ⊙ Apr-Nov; P ❄) This family-owned 1912 villa-turned-hotel has a classic, elegant facade with ochre paintwork and traditional green shutters. The rooms are brightly furnished with a yellow, blue and turquoise colour scheme, and shiny marble-clad bathrooms come complete with hot tub. The small balconies have forfeited the plastic for tasteful marble tables and have seamless sea views with Capri in the distance.

 **Eating**

Il Capriccio
ITALIAN €

(☎0974 84 52 41; Corso da Spiafriddo, Castellabate; meals €20-25; ⊙ noon-3pm & 7-11pm) On the road to Perdifumo, this is a favourite local choice. An unassuming place with a terrace, Il Capriccio has a gracious host in owner Enxo. The menu runs the gamut from seafood classics such as *zuppa di cozze* (mussel soup) and *polipetti affogati* (poached octopus) to less fishy options such as *zuppa di ceci* (chickpea soup).

★ Osteria del Borgo
CAMPANIAN €€

(☎0974 97 01 13; Via Roma 17, Pisciotta; meals €20-35; ⊙ noon-3pm & 7-11pm) From your perch on the stone terrace, you'll hear your order loudly repeated to the chef (ie Mamma), followed by the requisite banging of

pots and pans. In a land of simple food, this *osteria* (casual eatery) is an expert in making things uncomplicated, from the rustic bread to the scalding espresso via stalwart *primi* (first courses) where the prices rarely stray north of €10. You'll find it tucked away in Pisciotta's tight medieval labyrinth.

Arlecchino
SEAFOOD €€

(☎0974 96 18 89; Via Guglielmini, Santa Maria di Castellabate; pizzas from €4, meals €22-40; ⊙ noon-2.30pm & 7-11pm Mar-Nov; ⊕) Located across from the beach in the pretty southernmost part of Santa Maria, popular Arlecchino has picture windows overlooking the small sweep of sand. Packed to the gills at weekends, the restaurant primarily offers seafood, although the *ravioli salsa di noci* (ravioli in walnut sauce) gives the tuna and sea urchins a run for their money.

Palinuro

Palinuro is located in a picturesque bay sheltered by a promontory. Note that the majority of hotels and restaurants are seasonal and are only open from Easter to October.

◉ Sights & Activities

Aside from the grottoes, Palinuro is famous for its super-clean Blue Flag beaches. The centre of town is Piazza Virgilio, with a modern octagonal church (which looks transplanted from Salt Lake City), and main street Via Indipendenza, which is good for shopping and light eats.

Grotta Azzurra · CAVE

Although it doesn't have the hype of its Capri counterpart, Palinuro's Grotta Azzurra (Blue Grotto) is similarly spectacular, with a brilliant play of light and hue. It owes its name to the extraordinary effect created by the sunlight that filters inside from an underground passage lying at a depth of about 8m. Da Alessandro runs trips to this and other caves from €15.

Da Alessandro · BOATING

(📱347 6540931; www.costieradelcilento.it; Spiaggia del Porto di Palinuro; trips from €15; ⏱mid-Mar–mid-Nov) Located at a kiosk at the harbour, Da Alessandro runs boat trips to Palinuro's Grotta Azzurra as well as to Grotta Sulfurea, Grotta delle Ossa and Arco Naturale. Excursions also allow for a dip in the beautiful Baia del Buon Dormire. Kayak hire is available on the beach for €5 an hour.

🛏 Sleeping

Antico Maniero Palinuro · B&B €

(📱0974 93 30 38; www.anticomanieropalinuro.it; Colle San Sergio, Centola; s €50-100, d €60-110; ⏱Easter-Oct) Located in a stone mansion with a gorgeous terrace and sweeping sea views, Antico Maniero Palinuro features unashamedly romantic rooms – with drapes, lace bedspreads and dark-wood furniture – that stay on the right side of kitsch. Located between Centola and Palinuro, it's a good option if you're driving around the Cilento or along the coast.

Albergo Santa Caterina · HOTEL €€

(📱0974 93 10 19; www.albergosantacaterina.com; Via Indipendenza 53; d €100-155; ⏱Easter-Oct; P❄@🖭) At this superb hotel on the main street, guestroom colour schemes vary from brilliant canary yellow to deep Mediterranean blue. All have good-sized bathrooms, with baths as well as showers,

and private terraces. Sea views cost €20 more. The satellite TV here is a rare treat in these parts.

 Eating

O Guarracino · SEAFOOD €

(📱0974 93 83 09; www.oguarracino.it; Via Porto; meals €20-25; ⏱noon-3pm & 7pm-midnight May-Aug, noon-3pm Mar, Apr, Sep & Oct) This humble beachside eatery is run by a fishing family that still plies the waters in winter. Expect the freshest grilled fish: sea bream, sea bass, yellowtail, swordfish, tuna – it's a long list.

Ristorante Core a Core · ITALIAN €€

(📱0974 93 16 91; www.coreacorepalinuro.it; Via Piano Faracchio 13; meals €30-40; ⏱12.45-2.45pm & 8pm-midnight; 🚗) Ignore the cheesy heart-shaped sign: with its glorious garden setting and great reputation for seafood, Core a Core is your best bet in Palinuro. The *antipasti al mare* (€19.50) is superb, and there's a menu of proper kids' food. Book in advance – it's popular. The restaurant is a 15-minute uphill walk from the centre of Palinuro.

Ristorante Miramare · SEAFOOD €€

(📱0974 93 18 37; www.miramarepalinuro.it; Corso Pisacane 89; meals from €28; ⏱noon-3pm & 7-11.30pm) Enjoying a supreme position, with a broad terrace overlooking the turquoise sea and small adjacent sandy cove, this place is part of the same-name hotel. The menu is predominantly seafood-based and holds few surprises, although there is the odd nod to the international palate, including roast beef. Otherwise, *spaghetti alla vongole* (spaghetti with clams) is a safe bet.

ℹ Information

Tourist Office (📱0974 93 81 44; Piazza Virgilio; ⏱10am-12.30pm & 5-7pm Mon-Sat, 10am-12.30pm Sun) In the main square, the Pro Loco can provide a town map and general information.

ROAD TRIP ESSENTIALS

Italy Driving Guide

Italy's stunning natural scenery, comprehensive road network and passion for cars makes it a wonderful road-trip destination.

DRIVING LICENCE & DOCUMENTS

➡ All EU driving licences are recognised in Italy.

➡ Travellers from other countries should obtain an International Driving Permit (IDP) through their national automobile association. This should be carried with your licence; it is not a substitute for it.

When driving in Italy you are required to carry with you:

➡ The vehicle registration document

➡ Your driving licence

➡ Proof of third-party liability insurance

INSURANCE

➡ Third-party liability insurance is mandatory for all vehicles in Italy, including cars brought in from abroad.

➡ If driving an EU-registered vehicle, your home country insurance is sufficient. Ask your insurer for a European Accident Statement (EAS) form, which can simplify matters in the event of an accident.

➡ Residents of non-EU countries should contact their insurance company to see if they need a green card international insurance certificate.

➡ Hire agencies provide the minimum legal insurance, but you can supplement it if you choose.

HIRING A CAR

Car-hire agencies are widespread in Italy but prebooking costs less than hiring a car once you arrive in Italy. Online booking agency Rentalcars.com (www.rentalcars.com) compares the rates of numerous car-rental companies.

Some things to consider before renting:

➡ Bear in mind that a car is generally more hassle than it's worth in cities, so only hire one for the time you'll be on the open road.

➡ Consider vehicle size carefully. High fuel prices, extremely narrow streets and tight parking conditions mean that smaller is often better.

➡ Road signs can be iffy in remote areas, so consider booking and paying for satnav.

Driving Fast Facts

Right or left? Drive on the right

Manual or automatic? Mostly manual

Legal driving age 18

Top speed limit 130km/h (on autostradas)

Signature car Flaming red Ferrari or Fiat 500

Driving Tips

A representative of the Automobile Club d'Italia (ACI) offers these pearls to ease your way on Italian roads:

➡ Pay particular attention to the weather. In summer it gets very hot, but in winter watch out for ice, snow and fog.

➡ On the extra-urban roads and autostradas, cars must have their headlights on even during the day.

➡ Watch out for signs at the autostrada toll booths – the lanes marked 'Telepass' are for cars that pay through an automatic electronic system without stopping.

➡ Watch out in the cities – big and small – for the Limited Traffic Zones (ZTL) and pay parking. There is no universal system for indicating these or their hours.

➡ Many agencies have a minimum rental age of 25 and a maximum of 79. You can sometimes hire if you're over 21 but supplements will apply.

➡ To rent you'll need a credit card, valid driving licence (with IDP if necessary) and passport or photo ID. Note that some companies require that you've had your licence for at least a year.

➡ Hire cars come with the minimum legal insurance, which you can supplement by purchasing additional coverage.

➡ Check with your credit-card company to see if it offers a Collision Damage Waiver, which covers you for additional damage if you use that card to pay for the car.

The following companies have pickup locations throughout Italy:

Auto Europe (www.autoeurope.it)

Avis (www.avisautonoleggio.it)

Budget (www.budgetinternational.com)

Europcar (www.europcar.it)

Hertz (www.hertz.it)

Italy by Car (www.italybycar.it)

Maggiore (www.maggiore.it)

Sixt (www.sixt.it)

Motorcycles

Agencies throughout Italy rent motorbikes, ranging from small Vespas to large touring bikes. Prices start at around €35/150 per day/week for a 50cc scooter; upwards of €80/400 per day/week for a 650cc motorcycle.

BRINGING YOUR OWN VEHICLE

➡ All foreign vehicles entering Italy should display the nationality plate of its country of registration.

➡ If you're driving a left-hand-drive UK vehicle you'll have to adjust its headlights to avoid dazzling oncoming traffic.

➡ You'll need to carry snow chains in your car if travelling in mountainous areas between 15 October and 15 April.

MAPS

We recommend you purchase a good road map for your trip.

Touring Club Italiano (www.touringclub.com) The best driving maps, by Italy's largest map publisher. They are available at bookstores across Italy or online:

Stanfords (www.stanfords.co.uk) Excellent UK-based shop that stocks many useful maps.

Omni Resources (www.omnimap.com) US-based online retailer with an impressive selection of Italian maps.

ROAD CONDITIONS

Italy's extensive road network covers the entire peninsula and with enough patience you'll be able to get just about anywhere. Most roads are in good condition but a lack of maintenance in some areas means that you should be prepared for potholes and bumpy surfaces, particularly on smaller, secondary roads.

Traffic in and around the main cities is bad during morning and evening rush hours. Coastal roads get very busy on summer weekends. As a rule, traffic is quietest between 2pm and 4pm.

Road Categories

Autostradas Italy's toll-charging motorways. On road signs they're marked by a white 'A' and number on a green background. The main north–south artery is the A1, aka the Autostrada del Sole (the 'Motorway of the Sun'), which runs from Milan to Naples via Bologna, Florence and Rome. The main road south from Naples to Reggio di Calabria is the A3. To drive on an autostrada pick up a ticket at the entry barrier and pay (by cash or credit card) as you exit.

Strade statali (state highways) Represented on maps by 'S' or 'SS'. Vary from four-lane highways to two-lane roads. The latter can be extremely slow, especially in mountainous regions.

Strade regionali (regional highways) Like SS roads but administered by regional authorities rather than the state. Coded 'SR' or 'R'.

Strade provinciali (provincial highways) Smaller and slower roads. Coded 'SP' or 'P'.

Along with their A or SS number, some Italian roads are labelled with an E number – for example, the A4 autostrada is also shown as the E64 on maps and signs. This E number refers to the road's designation on the Europe-wide E-road network. E routes, which often cross national boundaries, are generally made up of major national roads strung together.

Limited Traffic Zones

Many Italian cities have designated their historic centres as Limited Traffic Zones (ZTL). These areas are off-limits to unauthorised vehicles and entry points are covered by street cameras. If you're caught entering one without the necessary permission you risk a fine. Being in a hire car will not exempt you from this rule. Contact your hotel or accommodation supplier if you think you'll need to access a ZTL.

Coins

Always try to keep some coins to hand. They come in very useful for parking meters.

Road Trip Websites

AUTOMOBILE ASSOCIATIONS

Automobile Club d'Italia (www.aci.it) Has a comprehensive online guide to motoring in Italy. Provides 24-hour roadside assistance.

CONDITIONS & TRAFFIC

Autostrade (www.autostrade.it) Comprehensive site with real time traffic info on Italy's motorways. Also lists service stations, petrol prices and toll costs.

CCISS (www.cciss.it) Italian-language site with updates on road works and real time traffic flows.

MAPS & ROUTE PLANNING

Michelin (www.viamichelin.it) Online road-trip planner.

Tutto Città (www.tuttocitta.it) Good for detailed town and city maps.

Mappy (https://en.mappy.com) Online mapping tool.

ROAD RULES

➡ Drive on the right; overtake on the left.

➡ It's obligatory to wear seat belts (front and rear), to drive with your headlights on outside built-up areas, and to carry a warning triangle and fluorescent waistcoat in case of breakdown.

➡ Wearing a helmet is compulsory on all two-wheeled vehicles.

➡ Motorbikes can enter most restricted traffic areas in Italian cities, and traffic police generally turn a blind eye to motorcycles or scooters parked on footpaths.

➡ The blood alcohol limit is 0.05%; it's zero for drivers under 21 and for those who have had their licence for less than three years.

Unless otherwise indicated, speed limits are as follows.

➡ 130km/h on autostradas
➡ 110km/h on main roads outside built-up areas
➡ 90km/h on secondary roads outside built-up areas
➡ 50km/h in built-up areas

Road Etiquette

➡ Italian drivers are fast, aggressive and skilful. Lane hopping and late braking are the norm and it's not uncommon to see cars tailgating at 130km/h. Don't expect cars to slow down for you or let you out. As soon as you see a gap, go for it. Italians expect the unexpected and react swiftly, but be decisive.

➡ Headlight flashing is common on the roads and has several meanings. If a car behind you flashes it means: 'Get out of the way' or 'Don't pull out, I'm not stopping'. But if an approaching car flashes you, it's warning you that there's a police check ahead.

➡ Use of the car horn is widespread. It might be a warning but it might equally be an expression of frustration at slow-moving traffic or celebration that the traffic light's just turned green.

PARKING

➡ Parking can be a major headache. Space is at a premium in towns and cities and Italy's traffic wardens are annoyingly efficient.

➡ Parking spaces outlined in blue are designated for paid parking – get a ticket from the nearest meter (coins only) or *tabaccaio* (tobacconist) and display it on your dashboard. Note that charges often don't apply overnight, typically between 8pm and 8am.

➡ White or yellow lines almost always indicate that residential permits are needed.

Driving Problem Buster

I can't speak Italian, will that be a problem? When at a petrol station you might have to ask the attendant for your fill-up. Ask for the amount you want, so *venti euro* for €20 or *pieno* for full. Always specify *benzina senza piombo* for unleaded petrol or *gasolio* for diesel.

What should I do if my car breaks down? Call the service number of your car-hire company. The Automobile Club d'Italia (ACI) provides 24-hour roadside assistance – call ☎803 116 from an Italian landline or mobile, or ☎800 116800 from a foreign mobile phone. Foreigners do not have to join but instead pay a per-incident fee. Note that in the event of a breakdown, a warning triangle is compulsory, as is use of an approved yellow or orange safety vest if you leave your vehicle.

What if I have an accident? For minor accidents there's no need to call the police. Fill in an accident report – *Constatazione Amichevole di Incidente* (CAI; Agreed Motor Accident Statement) – through your car-hire firm or insurance company.

What should I do if I get stopped by the police? The police will want to see your passport (or photo ID), licence, car registration papers and proof of insurance.

Will I need to pay tolls in advance? No. When you join an autostrada you have to pick up a ticket at the barrier. When you exit you pay based on the distance you've covered. Pay by cash or credit card.

Are the road signs easy to understand? Most signs are fairly obvious but it helps to know that town/city centres are indicated by the word *centro* and a kind of black-and-white bullseye sign; *divieto fermata* means 'no stopping'; and *tutte le direzione* means 'all directions'. See the inside back cover of this book for some of the most common road signs.

Will I be able to find ATMs along the road? Some autostrada service stations have ATMs (known as *bancomat* in Italian). Otherwise they are widely available in towns and cities.

FUEL

➡ Staffed filling stations *(benzinai, stazioni di servizio)* are widespread. Smaller stations tend to close between about 1pm and 3.30pm and sometimes also on Sunday afternoons.

➡ Many stations have self-service *(fai da te)* pumps that you can use 24 hours a day. To use one insert a banknote into the payment machine and press the number of the pump you want.

➡ Unleaded petrol is marked as *benzina senza piombo*; diesel as *gasolio*.

➡ Italy's petrol prices are among the highest in Europe and vary from one station to another. At the time of writing, unleaded petrol was averaging €1.46 per litre; diesel €1.29 per litre.

➡ At petrol stations, it costs slightly less to fill up yourself rather than have an assistant do it.

➡ Fuel costs more at austostrada service stations.

SAFETY

➡ The main safety threat to motorists is theft. Hire cars and foreign vehicles are a target for robbers and although you're unlikely to have a problem, thefts do occur.

➡ As a general rule, always lock your car and never leave anything showing, particularly valuables and certainly not overnight. If at all possible, avoid leaving luggage in a car.

➡ It's a good idea to pay extra to leave your car in supervised car parks.

RADIO

➡ RAI, Italy's state broadcaster, operates three national radio stations (Radiouno, Radiodue, Radiotre) offering news, current affairs, classical and commercial music.

➡ Isoradio, another RAI station, provides regular news and traffic bulletins.

Road Distances (KM)

Note
Distances between Palermo and mainland towns do not take into account the ferry from Reggio di Calabria to Messina. Add an extra hour to your journey time to allow for this crossing.

	Bari	Bologna	Florence	Genoa	Milan	Naples	Palermo	Perugia	Reggio di Calabria	Rome	Siena	Trento	Trieste	Turin	Venice
Bologna	681														
Florence	784	106													
Genoa	996	285	268												
Milan	899	218	324	156											
Naples	322	640	534	758	858										
Palermo	734	1415	1345	1569	1633	811									
Perugia	612	270	164	432	488	408	1219								
Reggio di Calabria	490	1171	1101	1325	1389	567	272	816							
Rome	482	408	302	526	626	232	1043	170	664						
Siena	714	176	70	296	394	464	1275	103	867	232					
Trento	892	233	339	341	218	874	1626	459	1222	641	375				
Trieste	995	308	414	336	420	948	1689	543	1445	715	484	279			
Turin	1019	338	442	174	139	932	1743	545	1307	702	460	349	551		
Venice	806	269	265	387	284	899	799	394	1296	567	335	167	165	415	
Verona	808	141	247	282	164	781	1534	377	1139	549	293	97	250	295	120

Italy Travel Guide

GETTING THERE & AWAY

AIR

The following are Italy's main international airports. Car hire is available at all these airports.

Rome Fiumicino (www.adr.it/fiumicino) Officially known as Leonardo da Vinci International Airport.

Rome Ciampino (www.adr.it/ciampino) Hub for Ryanair flights to Rome.

Milan Malpensa (www.milanomalpensa -airport.com)

Milan Linate (www.milanolinate-airport. com) Milan's second airport.

Venice Marco Polo (www.veniceairport.it)

Pisa International (www.pisa-airport.com) Main international gateway for Tuscany.

Naples International (www.aeroportodi napoli.it) Also known as Capodichino.

Catania Fontanarossa (www.aeroporto. catania.it) Sicily's busiest airport.

Bergamo Orio al Serio (www.orioaero porto.it) Used by European low-cost carriers.

Turin Caselle (www.aeroportoditorino.it)

Bologna Guglielmo Marconi (www. bologna-airport.it)

Bari Karol Wojtyła (www.aeroportidi puglia.it)

Palermo Falcone-Borsellino (www. gesap.it)

Cagliari Elmas (www.cagliariairport.it) Main gateway for Sardinia.

CAR & MOTORCYCLE

Driving into Italy is fairly straightforward – thanks to the Schengen Agreement, there are no customs checks when driving in from neighbours France, Switzerland, Austria and Slovenia.

Aside from the coastal roads linking Italy with France and Slovenia, border crossings into Italy mostly involve tunnels through the Alps (open year-round) or mountain passes (seasonally closed and requiring snow chains).

The list below outlines the major points of entry.

Austria From Innsbruck to Bolzano via A22/ E45 (Brenner Pass); Villach to Tarvisio via A23/E55.

France From Nice to Ventimiglia via A10/E80; Modane to Turin via A32/E70 (Fréjus Tunnel); Chamonix to Courmayeur via A5/E25 (Mont Blanc Tunnel).

Slovenia From Sežana to Trieste via SR58/E70.

Switzerland From Martigny to Aosta via SS27/E27 (Grand St Bernard Tunnel); Lugano to Como via A9/E35.

SEA

International car ferries sail to Italy from Albania, Croatia, France (Corsica), Greece, Malta, Montenegro, Morocco, Slovenia, Spain and Tunisia. Some routes only operate in summer, when ticket prices rise. Prices for vehicles vary according to their size. Car hire is not always available at ports, so check beforehand.

The helpful website www.directferries. co.uk allows you to search routes and compare prices between international ferry companies.

Principal operators include the following:

Adria Ferries (www.adriaferries.com) Albania to Bari (nine hours), Ancona (20 hours), Trieste (37 hours).

Anek Lines (www.anekitalia.com) Greece to Bari (eight to 18½ hours), Ancona (eight to 22 hours), Venice (25 to 32 hours).

GNV (Grandi Navi Veloci; www.gnv.it) Spain to Genoa (20 hours).

Grimaldi Lines (www.grimaldi-lines.com) Spain to Civitavecchia (20 hours), Savona (17 to 20 hours).

Jadrolinija (www.jadrolinija.hr) Croatia to Ancona (from nine hours), Bari (10 hours).

Minoan Lines (www.minoan.it) Greece to Ancona (17 to 23 hours).

Montenegro Lines (www.montenegrolines.net) Bar to Bari (10 hours).

Superfast (www.superfast.com) Greece to Bari (nine to 16 hours), Ancona (eight to 22 hours), Venice (14 to 33 hours).

TRAIN

Regular trains on two western lines connect Italy with France (one along the coast and the other from Turin into the French Alps). Trains from Milan head north into Switzerland and on towards the Benelux countries. Further east, two lines connect with Central and Eastern Europe.

Car hire is generally available at principal city stations.

➡ Airline companies will arrange assistance at airports if you notify them of your needs in advance. For help at Rome's Fiumicino or Ciampino airports contact ADR Assistance (www.adrassistance.it).

➡ Some taxis are equipped to carry passengers in wheelchairs; ask for a taxi for a *sedia a rotelle* (wheelchair).

➡ If you are driving, EU disabled parking permits are recognised in Italy, giving you the same parking rights that local drivers with disabilities have.

➡ If you have an obvious disability and/or appropriate ID, many museums and galleries offer free admission for yourself and a companion.

Resources include the following:

Village for All (www.villageforall.net/en) Performs on-site audits of tourist facilities in Italy and San Marino. Most of the 67 facilities are accommodation providers, ranging from camping grounds to high-class hotels.

Tourism without Barriers (www.turismo senzabarriere.it) Has a searchable database of accessible accommodation and tourist attractions in Tuscany, with a scattering of options in other regions.

Fondazione Cesare Serono (www.fondazioneserono.org/disabilita/spiagge -accessibili/spiagge-accessibili) A list (in Italian) of accessible beaches.

DIRECTORY A–Z

ACCESSIBLE TRAVEL

Italy is not an easy country for travellers with disabilities. Cobblestone streets and pavements blocked by parked cars and scooters make getting around difficult for wheelchair users. And while many buildings have lifts, they are not always wide enough for wheelchairs. Not a lot has been done to make life easier for hearing- or vision-impaired travellers either. However, awareness of accessibility issues and a culture of inclusion are steadily growing.

➡ The Italian National Tourist Office in your country may be able to provide advice on Italian associations for travellers with disabilities and information on what help is available.

Practicalities

Smoking Banned in enclosed public spaces, which includes restaurants, bars, shops and public transport.

Time Italy uses the 24-hour clock and is on Central European Time, one hour ahead of GMT/UTC.

TV The main terrestrial channels are Rai 1, 2 and 3 run by Rai (www.rai.it), Italy's state-owned national broadcaster, and Canale 5, Italia 1 and Rete 4 run by Mediaset (www.mediaset.it).

Weights & Measures Italy uses the metric system, so kilometres not miles, litres not gallons.

Accommodation Tax

➡ Italy's *tassa di soggiorno* (accommodation tax) sees visitors charged an extra €1 to €7 per night as a 'room occupancy tax'.

➡ Exactly how much you're charged depends on the type of accommodation (campground, guesthouse, hotel), a hotel's star rating, and the number of people under your booking.

➡ Our listings do not include the hotel tax, although it's always a good idea to confirm whether taxes are included when booking.

Download Lonely Planet's free Accessible Travel guide from http://shop.lonely planet.com/accessible-travel.

ACCOMMODATION

From dreamy villas to chic boutique hotels, historic hideaways and ravishing farm stays *(agriturismi)*, Italy offers accommodation to suit every taste and budget.

Seasons & Rates

The following price ranges refer to a double room with private bathroom (breakfast included) in high season.

€ less than €110

€€ €110–200

€€€ more than €200

Accommodation rates fluctuate enormously from high to low season, and even from day to day depending on demand, season and booking method (online, through an agency etc).

Book Your Stay Online

For more accommodation reviews by Lonely Planet authors, check out http://hotels.lonelyplanet.com. You'll find independent reviews, as well as recommendations on the best places to stay. Best of all, you can book online.

As a rule, peak rates apply at Easter, in summer (July and August) and over the Christmas/New Year period. But there are exceptions – in the mountains, high season means the ski season (December to late March). Also, August is high season on the coast but low season in many cities where hotels offer discounts.

Southern Italy is generally cheaper than the north.

Reservations

➡ Always book ahead in peak season, even if it's only for the first night or two.

➡ Reserving a room is essential during key festivals and events when demand is very high.

➡ In the off-season, it always pays to call ahead to check that a hotel is open. Many coastal hotels close for winter, typically opening from late March or Easter to late October.

➡ Hotels usually require that reservations be confirmed with a credit-card number. No-shows will be docked one night's accommodation.

B&Bs

B&Bs are a burgeoning sector of the Italian accommodation market and can be found throughout the country in both urban and rural settings. Options include everything from restored farmhouses, city *palazzi* (mansions) and seaside bungalows to rooms in family houses. In some cases, a B&B can also refer to a self-contained apartment with basic breakfast provisions provided. Tariffs for a double room cover a wide range, from around €60 to €140.

Hotels & Pensioni

While the difference between an *albergo* (hotel) and a *pensione* is often minimal, a *pensione* will generally be of one- to three-star quality while an *albergo* can be awarded up to five stars. *Locande* (inns) long fell into much the same category as *pensioni*, but the term has become a trendy one in some parts and reveals little about the quality of a place. *Affittacamere* are simple rooms for rent in private houses.

All hotels are rated from one to five stars:

➡ One-star hotels and *pensioni* tend to be basic and often do not offer private bathrooms.

➡ Two-star places are similar but rooms will generally have a private bathroom.

→ Three-star hotel rooms will come with a hairdryer, minibar (or fridge), safe and air-con.

→ Four- and five-star hotels offer facilities such as room service, laundry and dry-cleaning.

Tourist offices usually have booklets with local accommodation listings. Many hotels are also signing up with online accommodation-booking services.

Agriturismi

From rustic country houses to luxurious estates and fully functioning farms, Italian farm stays, known as *agriturismi* (singular – *agriturismo*) are hugely popular. Comfort levels, facilities and prices vary but the best will offer swimming pools and top-class accommodation. Many also operate restaurants specialising in traditional local cuisine.

For listings and further details, check the following:

Agriturismo.it (www.agriturismo.it)

Agriturismo.net (www.agriturismo.net)

Agriturismo.com (www.agriturismo.com)

Agriturismo-Italia.net (www.agriturismo-italia.net)

Other Options

Camping A popular summer option. Most campsites are big, summer-only complexes with swimming pools, restaurants and supermarkets. Many have space for RVs and offer bungalows or simple, self-contained flats. Minimum stays sometimes apply in high season. Check out www.campeggi.com and www.camping.it.

Hostels Official HI hostels and a growing contingent of independent hostels offer dorm beds and private rooms. Breakfast is usually included in rates and dinner is sometimes available for about €10 to €15. For listings and further details, see www.aighostels.com or www.hostelworld.com.

Convents & Monasteries Some convents and monasteries provide basic accommodation. Expect curfews, few frills and value for money. Useful resources include www.stpatricksamericanrome.org and www.initaly.com/agri/convents.htm.

Refuges Mountain huts *(rifugi)* with rooms sleeping anything from two to a dozen or more people. Many also offer hot meals and/or communal cooking facilities. Generally open from June to late September.

Villas Villas and *fattorie* (farmhouses) can be rented in their entirety or sometimes by the room. Many have swimming pools.

ELECTRICITY

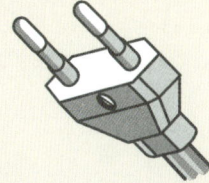

Type C
220V/50Hz

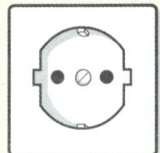

Type F
230V/50Hz

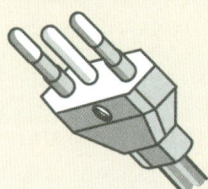

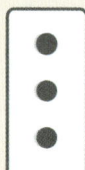

Type L
220V/50Hz

FOOD

A full Italian meal consists of an antipasto (appetiser), *primo* (first course, usually a pasta, risotto or polenta), *secondo* (second course, meat or fish) with *contorno* (vegetable side dish) or *insalata* (salad), and *dolce* (dessert) and/or fruit. When eating out it's perfectly OK to mix and match and order, say, a *primo* followed by an *insalata* or *contorno*.

Where to Eat

Italy has no shortage of eating options, and reserving a table on the day of your meal is usually fine. Top-end restaurants

may need to be booked a month or more in advance, while popular eateries in tourist areas should be booked at least a few days ahead in peak season.

Ristorante (Restaurant) Formal dining, often with comprehensive wine lists and more sophisticated local or national fare.

Trattoria Informal, family-run restaurant cooking up traditional regional dishes. Generally cheap to midrange.

Osteria Similar to a trattoria, with a focus on traditional cooking.

Enoteca Wine bars invariably double as a casual place to graze or dine, typically serving snacks such as cheese, cold meats, bruschette and *crostini* (little toasts) to accompany your tipple.

Agriturismo A farmhouse offering food made with farm-grown produce. Booking generally required.

Pizzeria Alongside pizza, many pizzerias also offer antipasti, pastas, meat and vegetable dishes. They're often only open in the evening. The best have a wood oven (*forno a legna*).

Bar & Cafe Italians often breakfast on a *cornetto* (Italian croissant) and cappuccino at a bar or cafe. Many places sell *panini* (bread rolls with simple fillers) at lunchtime and serve a buffet of hot and cold dishes during the early evening *aperitivo* (aperitif) hour.

Market Most towns and cities have morning produce markets where you can stock up on picnic provisions.

HEALTH

➡ Italy has a public health system (*Servizio Sanitario Nazionale, SSN*) that is legally bound to provide emergency care to everyone.

➡ EU nationals are entitled to reduced-cost, sometimes free, medical care with a European Health Insurance Card (EHIC), available from your home health authority.

➡ Non-EU citizens should take out medical insurance.

➡ For emergency treatment, go to the *pronto soccorso* (casualty department) of an *ospedale* (public hospital), though be prepared for a long wait.

➡ Pharmacists can give advice and sell over-the-counter medication for minor illnesses.

Eating Price Ranges

The following price ranges refer to a two-course meal with a glass of house wine and *coperto* (cover charge).

€ less than €25

€€ €25–45

€€€ more than €45

Note that most eating establishments add a *coperto* of around €2 to €3. Some also include a service charge (*servizio*) of 10% to 15%.

➜ Pharmacies typically open from 8.30am to 7.30pm Monday to Friday and on Saturday mornings. Outside these hours, they open on a rotational basis. When closed, a pharmacy is legally required to post a list of places open in the vicinity.

➜ In larger cities, English-speaking doctors are often available for house calls or appointments through private clinics.

➜ Italian tap water is fine to drink.

➜ No vaccinations are required for travel to Italy.

LGBT+ TRAVELLERS

➜ Homosexuality is legal in Italy and even widely accepted in the major cities. However, discretion is still wise and overt displays of affection by LGBT+ couples can attract a negative response, especially in smaller towns.

➜ There are gay venues in Rome, Milan and Bologna, and a handful in places such as Florence and Naples. Some coastal towns and resorts (such as the Tuscan town of Viareggio or Taormina in Sicily) have much more action in summer.

Resources include the following:

Arcigay (www.arcigay.it) Bologna-based national organisation for the LGBT+ community.

Gay.it (www.gay.it) Website featuring LGBT+ news, features and gossip.

Pride (www.prideonline.it) Culture, politics, travel and health with an LGBT+ focus.

INTERNET ACCESS

➜ Free wi-fi is widely available in hotels, hostels, B&Bs and *agriturismi,* though signal quality varies. Some places also provide laptops/computers.

➜ Many bars and cafes offer free wi-fi.

➜ Numerous Italian cities and towns offer public wi-fi hotspots, including Rome, Milan, Bologna, Florence and Venice. To use them, you'll need to register online using a credit card or an Italian mobile number.

➜ A free smartphone app, wifi.italia.it, allows you to connect to participating networks through a single login. Released in summer 2017, it gets mixed reports.

MONEY

Italy uses the euro. Euro notes come in denominations of €500, €200, €100, €50, €20, €10 and €5; coins come in denominations of €2 and €1, and 50, 20, 10, five, two and one cents.

For the latest exchange rates, check out www.xe.com.

Admission Prices

➜ State museums and sites offer free admission to under-18s and discounted entry to 18 to 25 year olds.

➜ You'll need photo ID to claim reduced entry.

➜ State-run museums are free on the first Sunday of the month between October and March.

ATMs & Credit Cards

➜ ATMs (known as *bancomat*) are widely available throughout Italy and most will accept cards tied into the Visa, MasterCard, Cirrus and Maestro systems.

➜ Credit cards such as Visa, MasterCard, Eurocard, Cirrus and Eurocheques are widely accepted. Amex is also recognised, though less common.

➜ Virtually all midrange and top-end hotels accept credit cards, as do most restaurants and large shops. Some cheaper *pensioni,*

Tipping Guide

Italians are not big tippers. The following is a rough guide.

Taxis Optional, but most round up to the nearest euro.

Hotels Tip porters about €5 at high-end hotels.

Restaurants Service (*servizio*) is generally included – otherwise, a euro or two is fine in pizzerias and trattorias, and 5% to 10% in smart restaurants.

Bars Not necessary, although many leave small change if drinking coffee at the bar, usually €0.10 or €0.20.

trattorias and pizzerias only accept cash. Don't rely on credit cards at smaller museums or galleries.

➡ Always inform your bank of your travel plans to avoid your card being blocked for payments made in unusual locations.

➡ Check any charges with your bank. Most banks charge a foreign exchange fee as well as a transaction charge of around 1% to 3%.

➡ If your card is lost, stolen or swallowed by an ATM, call to have it blocked:

Amex ☑06 7290 0347
Diners Club ☑800 393939
MasterCard ☑800 870866
Visa ☑800 819014

Moneychangers

➡ You can change money at a *cambio* (exchange office) or post office. Some banks might change money, though many now only do this for account holders. Post offices and banks offer the best rates; exchange offices keep longer hours, but watch for high commissions and inferior rates.

➡ Take your passport or photo ID when exchanging money.

Italian Wine Classifications

Italian wines are classified according to strict quality-control standards and carry one of four denominations:

DOCG (*Denominazione di Origine Controllata e Garantita*) Italy's best wines; made in specific areas according to stringent production rules.

DOC (*Denominazione di Origine Controllata*) Quality wines produced in defined regional areas.

IGT (*Indicazione di Geografica Tipica*) Wines typical of a certain region.

Vino da Tavola Wines for everyday drinking; often served as house wine in trattorias.

OPENING HOURS

Opening hours vary throughout the year. We've provided high-season hours, which are generally in use over summer. Summer refers to the period between April and September (or October); winter is October (or November) to March.

Banks 8.30am to 1.30pm and 2.45pm to 4.30pm Monday to Friday

Bars & cafes 7.30am to 8pm, sometimes to 1am or 2am

Clubs 10pm to 4am or 5am

Restaurants noon to 3pm and 7.30pm to 11pm (later in summer)

Shops 9am to 1pm and 3.30pm to 7.30pm (or 4pm to 8pm) Monday to Saturday. In main cities some shops stay open at lunchtime and on Sunday mornings. Some shops close Monday mornings.

PUBLIC HOLIDAYS

Most Italians take their annual holiday in August. Many businesses and shops close for at least part of the month, particularly around *Ferragosto* (Feast of the Assumption) on 15 August.

Individual towns have public holidays to celebrate the feasts of their patron saints. National public holidays include the following:

Capodanno (New Year's Day) 1 January

Epifania (Epiphany) 6 January

Pasquetta (Easter Monday) March/April

Giorno della Liberazione (Liberation Day) 25 April

Festa del Lavoro (Labour Day) 1 May

Festa della Repubblica (Republic Day) 2 June

Ferragosto (Feast of the Assumption) 15 August

Festa di Ognisanti (All Saints' Day) 1 November

Festa dell'Immacolata Concezione (Feast of the Immaculate Conception) 8 December

Natale (Christmas Day) 25 December

Festa di Santo Stefano (Boxing Day) 26 December

SAFE TRAVEL

Italy is a safe country but petty theft can be a problem. There's no need for paranoia but be aware that thieves and pickpockets operate in touristy areas, so watch out when exploring the sights in Rome, Florence, Venice and Naples.

Cars, particularly those with foreign number plates or rental-company stickers, provide rich pickings for thieves.

In case of theft or loss, report the incident to the police within 24 hours and ask for a statement.

Some tips:

➡ Wear your bag/camera strap across your body and away from the road – thieves on mopeds can swipe a bag and be gone in seconds.

➡ Never drape your bag over an empty chair at a street-side cafe or put it where you can't see it. Also, never leave valuables in coat pockets in restaurants or other places with communal coat hooks.

➡ Always check your change to see you haven't been short changed.

TELEPHONE

Domestic Calls

➡ Italian area codes begin with 0 and consist of up to four digits. They are an integral part of all phone numbers and must be dialled even when calling locally.

➡ Mobile-phone numbers begin with a three-digit prefix starting with 3.

➡ Toll-free numbers are known as *numeri verdi* and usually start with 800.

➡ Some six-digit national rate numbers are also in use (such as those for Alitalia and Trenitalia).

International Calls

➡ To call Italy from abroad, dial your country's international access code, then Italy's country code (39) followed by the area code of the location you want (including the first zero) and the rest of the number.

➡ To call abroad from Italy dial 00, then the country code, followed by the full number.

➡ Avoid making international calls from hotels, as rates are high.

➡ The cheapest way to call is to use an app such as Skype or Viber, connecting through the wi-fi at your hotel, B&B etc.

Mobile Phones

➡ Italian mobile phones operate on the GSM 900/1800 network, which is compatible with the rest of Europe and Australia but not always with the North American GSM or CDMA systems – check with your service provider.

➡ The cheapest way of using your mobile is to buy a prepaid *(prepagato)* Italian SIM card. TIM *(Telecom Italia Mobile;* www.tim.it), Wind (www.wind.it), Vodafone (www.vodafone.it) and Tre (www.tre.it) all offer SIM cards and have retail outlets across the country. You can then top up as you go, either online or at one of your provider's shops.

➡ Note that by Italian law all SIM cards must be registered in Italy, so make sure you have your passport or ID card when you buy one.

TOILETS

Besides in museums, galleries, train stations and autostrada service stations, there are few public toilets in Italy. If you're caught short, the best thing to do is to nip into a cafe or bar. The polite thing to do is to order something at the bar.

You may need to pay to use some public toilets (usually €0.50 to €1.50).

Important Numbers

Italy country code (☏39)

International access code (☏00)

Police (☏112, 113)

Ambulance (☏118)

Fire (☏115)

Roadside assistance (☏803 116 from an Italian landline or mobile phone; ☏800 116800 from a foreign mobile phone)

TOURIST INFORMATION

➡ Italy's national tourist board, ENIT – Agenzia Nazionale del Turismo – has offices across the world. Its website, www.italia.it, provides both practical information and inspirational travel ideas.

➡ Most cities and towns in Italy have a tourist office that can provide maps, lists of local accommodation, and information on sights in the area.

➡ In larger towns and major tourist areas, English is generally spoken, along with other languages, depending on the region (for example, German in Alto Adige, French in Valle d'Aosta).

➡ Most tourist offices will respond to written or telephone requests for information.

➡ Office hours vary: in major tourist destinations, offices generally open daily, especially in the summer high season. In smaller centres, they generally observe regular office hours and open Monday to Friday, perhaps also on Saturday mornings.

➡ Affiliated information booths (at train stations and airports, for example) may keep slightly different hours.

➡ Tourist offices in Italy go under a variety of names, depending on who they're administered by (the local municipality, province or region), but most perform similar functions. On the ground, look for signs to the *Ufficio Turistico*.

Regional Tourist Authorities

Regional offices are generally more concerned with marketing and promotion than offering a public information service. However, they have useful websites.

Abruzzo (www.abruzzoturismo.it)
Basilicata (www.basilicataturistica.it)
Calabria (www.turiscalabria.it)
Campania (www.incampania.com)
Emilia-Romagna (www.emiliaromagna turismo.it)
Friuli Venezia Giulia (www.turismo.fvg.it)
Lazio (www.visitlazio.com)
Le Marche (www.turismo.marche.it)
Liguria (www.lamialiguria.it)
Lombardy (www.in-lombardia.it)
Molise (www.visitmolise.eu)
Piedmont (www.piemonteitalia.eu)
Puglia (www.viaggiareinpuglia.it)
Sardinia (www.sardegnaturismo.it)
Sicily (www.visitsicily.info)
Trentino-Alto Adige (www.visittrentino.it)
Tuscany (www.visittuscany.com)
Umbria (www.umbriatourism.it)
Valle d'Aosta (www.lovevda.it)
Veneto (www.veneto.eu)

VISAS

➡ Italy is one of the 26 European countries making up the Schengen area. There are no customs controls when travelling between Schengen countries, so the visa rules that apply to Italy apply to all Schengen countries.

➡ EU citizens do not need a visa to enter Italy.

➡ Nationals of some countries, including Australia, Canada, Israel, Japan, New Zealand, Switzerland and the USA, do not need a visa for stays of up to 90 days.

➡ Nationals of other countries will need a Schengen tourist visa – to check requirements see www.schengenvisainfo.com/tourist -schengen-visa.

➡ All non-EU and non-Schengen nationals entering Italy for more than 90 days or for any reason other than tourism (such as study or work) may need a specific visa. Check http://vistoperitalia.esteri.it for details.

➡ Ensure your passport is valid for at least six months beyond your departure date from Italy.

Language

Italian sounds can all be found in English. If you read our coloured pronunciation guides as if they were English, you'll be understood. Note that ai is pronounced as in 'aisle', ay as in 'say', ow as in 'how', dz as the 'ds' in 'lids', and that r is strong and rolled. If the consonant is written as a double letter, it's pronounced a little stronger, eg *sonno son·no* (sleep) versus *sono so·no* (I am). The stressed syllables are indicated with italics.

BASICS

Hello.	*Buongiorno.*	bwon·*jor*·no
Goodbye.	*Arrivederci.*	a·ree·ve·*der*·chee
Yes./No.	*Sì./No.*	see/no
Excuse me.	*Mi scusi.*	mee skoo·zee
Sorry.	*Mi dispiace.*	mee dees·*pya*·che
Please.	*Per favore.*	per fa·*vo*·re
Thank you.	*Grazie.*	*gra*·tsye

You're welcome.
Prego.　　　　　　　　pre·go

Do you speak English?
Parli inglese?　　　　par·lee een·*gle*·ze

I don't understand.
Non capisco.　　　　non ka·*pee*·sko

How much is this?
Quanto costa questo?　*kwan*·to *kos*·ta *kwe*·sto

ACCOMMODATION

Do you have a room?
Avete una camera?　　a·ve·te oo·na *ka*·me·ra

How much is it per night/person?
Quanto costa per　　　*kwan*·to *kos*·ta per
una notte/persona?　　oo·na *no*·te/per·*so*·na

DIRECTIONS

Where's ...?
Dov'è ...?　　　　　　do·ve ...

Can you show me (on the map)?
Può mostrarmi　　　　pwo mos·*trar*·mee
(sulla pianta)?　　　　(soo·la *pyan*·ta)

EATING & DRINKING

What would you recommend?
Cosa mi consiglia?　　*ko*·za mee kon·*see*·lya

I'd like ..., please.
Vorrei ..., per favore.　vo·*ray* ... per fa·*vo*·re

I don't eat (meat).
Non mangio (carne).　non *man*·jo (*kar*·ne)

Please bring the bill.
Mi porta il conto,　　mee *por*·ta eel *kon*·to
per favore?　　　　　per fa·*vo*·re

EMERGENCIES

Help!
Aiuto!　　　　　　　a·*yoo*·to

I'm lost.
Mi sono perso/a. (m/f)　mee so·no *per*·so/a

I'm ill.
Mi sento male.　　　mee *sen*·to ma·le

Call the police!
Chiami la polizia!　　kya·mee la po·lee·*tsee*·a

Call a doctor!
Chiami un medico!　　kya·mee oon me·dee·ko

Want More?

For in-depth language information and handy phrases, check out Lonely Planet's *Italian Phrasebook*. You'll find it at **shop.lonelyplanet.com**, or you can buy Lonely Planet's iPhone phrasebooks at the Apple App Store.

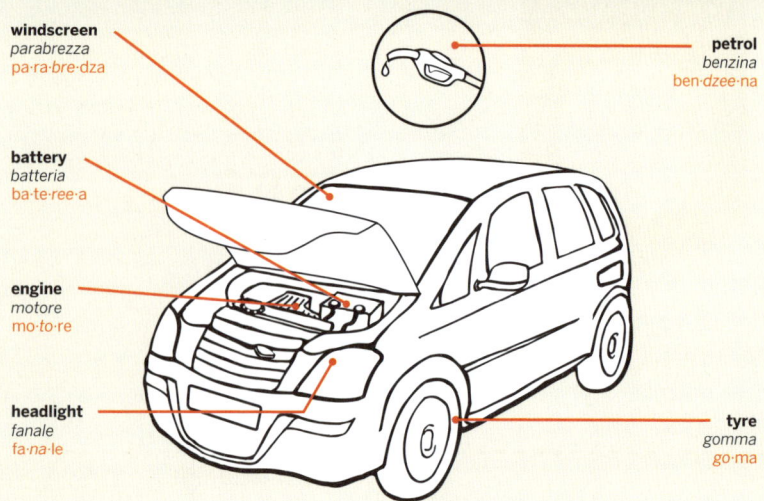

windscreen
parabrezza
pa·ra·bre·dza

petrol
benzina
ben·dzee·na

battery
batteria
ba·te·ree·a

engine
motore
mo·to·re

headlight
fanale
fa·na·le

tyre
gomma
go·ma

ON THE ROAD

I'd like to hire a/an ...	*Vorrei noleggiare ...*	vo·ray no·le·ja·re ...
4WD	*un fuoristrada*	oon fwo·ree·stra·da
automatic/ manual	*una macchina automatica/ manuale*	oo·na ma·kee·na ow·to·ma·tee·ka/ ma·noo·a·le
motorbike	*una moto*	oo·na mo·to
How much is it ...?	*Quanto costa ...?*	kwan·to kos·ta ...
daily	*al giorno*	al jor·no
weekly	*alla settimana*	a·la se·tee·ma·na

Does that include insurance?
E' compresa l'assicurazione?
e kom·pre·sa la·see·koo·ra·tsyo·ne

Does that include mileage?
E' compreso il chilometraggio?
e kom·pre·so eel kee·lo·me·tra·jo

What's the city/country speed limit?
Qual'è il limite di velocità in città/campagna?
kwa·le lee·mee·te dee ve·lo·chee·ta een chee·ta/kam·pa·nya

Is this the road to (Venice)?
Questa strada porta a (Venezia)?
kwe·sta stra·da por·ta a (ve·ne·tsya)

(How long) Can I park here?
(Per quanto tempo) Posso parcheggiare qui?
(per kwan·to tem·po) po·so par·ke·ja·re kwee

Please fill it up.
Il pieno, per favore.
eel pye·no per fa·vo·re

Where's a service station?
Dov'è una stazione di servizio?
do·ve oo·na sta·tsyo·ne dee ser·vee·tsyo

I'd like (30) litres.
Vorrei (trenta) litri.
vo·ray (tren·ta) lee·tree

Please check the oil/water.
Può controllare l'olio/ l'acqua, per favore?
pwo kon·tro·la·re lo·lyo/ la·kwa per fa·vo·re

I need a mechanic.
Ho bisogno di un meccanico.
o bee·zo·nyo dee oon me·ka·nee·ko

The car/motorbike has broken down.
La macchina/moto si è guastata.
la ma·kee·na/mo·to see e gwas·ta·ta

I had an accident.
Ho avuto un incidente.
o a·voo·to oon een·chee·den·te

Signs

Alt	Stop
Dare la Precedenza	Give Way
Deviazione	Detour
Divieto di Accesso	No Entry
Entrata	Entrance
Pedaggio	Toll
Senso Unico	One Way
Uscita	Exit

BEHIND THE SCENES

SEND US YOUR FEEDBACK

We love to hear from travellers – your comments help make our books better. We read every word, and we guarantee that your feedback goes straight to the authors. Visit **lonelyplanet. com/contact** to submit your updates and suggestions.

Note: We may edit, reproduce and incorporate your comments in Lonely Planet products such as guidebooks, websites and digital products, so let us know if you don't want your comments reproduced or your name acknowledged. For a copy of our privacy policy visit lonelyplanet.com/privacy.

ACKNOWLEDGMENTS

Climate map data adapted from Peel MC, Finlayson BL & McMahon TA (2007) 'Updated World Map of the Köppen-Geiger Climate Classification', *Hydrology and Earth System Sciences*, 11, 1633–44.

Illustration pp68–9 by Javier Zarracina

Cover photographs: Front: Atrani, Anna Biancoloto/ Shutterstock ©; Back: Ravello, Aygul Sarvarova/ Shutterstock ©

THIS BOOK

This 2nd edition of *Amalfi Coast Road Trips* was researched and written by Cristian Bonetto and Brendan Sainsbury. The previous edition was written by Cristian, Duncan Garwood, Paula Hardy, Robert Landon and Helena Smith. This guidebook was produced by the following:

Destination Editor Anna Tyler

Senior Product Editor Elizabeth Jones

Regional Senior Cartographer Anthony Phelan

Product Editor Katie Connolly

Book Designer Gwen Cotter

Assisting Editors Gabrielle Stefanos, Fionnuala Twomey, Simon Williamson

Cover Researcher Meri Blazevski

Thanks to Will Allen, Imogen Bannister, Sasha Baskett, Alexandra Bruzzese, Gemma Graham, Martin Heng, Jenna Myers, Kirsten Rawlings, Joe Revill, Sophia Seymour, Jo-Ann Titmarsh, Brana Vladisavljevic

OUR STORY

A beat-up old car, a few dollars in the pocket and a sense of adventure. In 1972 that's all Tony and Maureen Wheeler needed for the trip of a lifetime – across Europe and Asia overland to Australia. It took several months, and at the end – broke but inspired – they sat at their kitchen table writing and stapling together their first travel guide, *Across Asia on the Cheap.* Within a week they'd sold 1500 copies. Lonely Planet was born.

Today, Lonely Planet has offices in Franklin, London, Melbourne, Oakland, Dublin, Beijing and Delhi, with more than 600 staff and writers. We share Tony's belief that 'a great guidebook should do three things: inform, educate and amuse'.

INDEX

000 Map pages

000 Map pages

INDEX **R-W**

OUR WRITERS

CRISTIAN BONETTO

Despite being the son of northern Italians, Cristian has an enduring weakness for Naples and Campania. It took one visit as a young backpacker to get him hooked, and the Australian-born writer has been covering the region's food, culture and lifestyle for more than a decade. According to Cristian, no Italian city quite matches Naples' complexity and intrigue, and its ability to constantly surprise and contradict makes it a thrill to write about. The writer's musings have appeared in publications across the globe, and his Naples-based play *Il Cortile* (The Courtyard) has toured numerous Italian cities. Cristian has contributed to more than 30 Lonely Planet guides, including *Venice & the Veneto*, *New York City*, *Denmark* and *Singapore*. You can follow Cristian's adventures on Twitter (@CristianBonetto) and on Instagram (@rexcat75).

BRENDAN SAINSBURY

Born and raised in the UK in a town that never merits a mention in any guidebook (Andover, Hampshire), Brendan spent the holidays of his youth caravanning in the English Lake District and didn't leave Blighty until he was 19. Making up for lost time, he's since squeezed 70 countries into a sometimes precarious existence as a writer and professional vagabond. In the last 12 years, he has written more than 40 books for Lonely Planet from Castro's Cuba to the canyons of Peru.

Published by Lonely Planet Global Limited
CRN 554153
2nd edition – Jun 2020
ISBN 978 1 78657 568 5
© Lonely Planet 2020   Photographs © as indicated 2020
10 9 8 7 6 5 4 3 2 1
Printed in China